Jobs, Jobs, Jobs, Jobs:
Work in *Turbulent* Times

Your Own Work Action Plan!

Bruce B. Razban,   CEO, RI International, Inc.

Walter Kleine,   Pulitzer Prize nominee

Mark C. Fairbanks,   VP

Ed Seaman,   US Marine Corps, VP

Ron Leaf,   Attorney at law (Ret.)

This book will empower and inspire you to succeed in finding and keeping careers, jobs, and thriving work life in a turbulent world after Global Financial Crisis!

Based on more than three decades of management and technology consulting, I will show you how to be CEO of your life and career to succeed and never give up a few minutes before a miracle.

This book contains expert advice that is spelled out in practical and effective steps that will almost instantly optimize your job, career, and even life.

CHAPTERS:

Introduction

APPENDICES:

A: Executive Summary

B: Mr. Razban's Report to the White House Job Creation Committee as a Silicon Valley Community Leader

C: Work Action Plan for American Economy Regarding Job Creation

D: "General Commander" Warren Buffett Declares War on unemployment

E: "General Commander" Professor David Cheriton of Stanford University Starts American Googelar Production Line Innovation Manufacturing (GP-LIM)!

F: "General Commander" of FedEx Duplicates FedEx to Save American Jobs (JobEx)!

G: Similarities between Present Unemployment Situation and Vietnam War

H: **STOP ORDER!**

I: Living and Working in Constant Crisis, and Unemployment

J: What is Exactly Meant by Value-Add and Triple-Decker Career Bus?

K: Rolling in the Deep; We Could Have Had it All!

L: It Seems Just Like Yesterday and Barclay Simpson's Nine Principles of Business

M: Dollarization of Work-Life Balance Value

N: Work Action Plan for You and Me During Turbulent Economy

O: 1%, 4%, 99%, and 107.8%

P: Laid Off Banker Liberates Himself by Selling Frankfurters

Q: Ageism Rageism!

R: Abject Executive Poverty

S: Beware of Unemployment, Underemployment, Unhappy Employment Spillover to Relationships and Life

T: It was Mismanagement that got us into Global Financial Crisis; it is Management that will get us Out of It!

U: "This Was a Flat Spin! It would Have Scared Me Too!"

V: "General Commander" Howard Schultz of Starbucks

W: "Sheriff of Wall Street" in Michael Krazny's KQED Forum Program

X Digital Humanity, Integrity, and Code of Global Operational Ethics

Y: You have Only You and Only One Life to Live!

Z: Special Things Live on and on!

Please Contact: <u>bruce@razban.com</u>

DEDICATIONS:

This book is dedicated to my wife, daughter, brother, and sister. Without their love I could not have ever accomplished much!

Please Contact: <u>bruce@razban.com</u>

THANKS:

I owe a great deal to:
- Google.com and Google images that made research for this book fast, accurate, and painless.

- Debra Benton, who is a New York Times best seller. As always, has been a source of inspiration, guidance, and hope!

- Many from Stanford University, University of Wisconsin–Madison, London School of Economics (LSE), Sorbonne University in Paris, Technion in Israel, and others helped me during years of writing this book.

Please Contact: bruce@razban.com

Introduction:

One stormy and frigid February late afternoon in 2010, which looked just like a dark night, I found myself struggling with a lingering flu and at the same time trying to do my job of selling cars. Even with a fever that had resulted from the flu, I had to hang on to my job as if my life depended on it. However, what kept me going was that I knew that I was willing and able to help inspire others with jobs, careers, and life. After all, I had been unemployed as well as extremely successfully employed. I had firsthand experience with being hopelessly unemployed; I knew what being unhappily employed was like; I knew what being happily employed meant. I had experienced and walked the talk.

It was painfully true that I had had an excellent career as a senior management and technology consultant in Silicon Valley. Nevertheless now as a car salesman, I had to sell at least ten cars monthly to survive in this job! I was proud for doing the job for that moment, and not getting fired. However, for the former director that I was, this job was a sharp decline in comparison. When I lost my director level job, I had witnessed several colleagues go to the manager's office and come out packing after being fired for not having sold those ten cars for that month.

It was ironic that in a previous occasion I was reporting to the General Manager in this location and as a senior IT consultant I was making three to four times more money. But now this was a desperation job and the only job that I could after a long time of being unemployed.

This was the height of Global Financial Crisis, and after two years of unemployment I was lucky to have this job; in fact, I was lucky to have *any* job! So many of my colleagues had lost their jobs that I could not keep an accurate count.

I had begged and borrowed, but to my credit did not steal, from family, friends, and colleagues to survive financially. As ashamed as I was about begging, as senior management I had done that before. However, that was begging venture capitalists and for millions of dollars. I had never begged friends for $20 to be able to put gas in my car so as not to be stranded.

Was this all there was left of my disintegrated career? What happened to thirty years of devoted service to several major

8

corporations and start-ups? Was this the deserving reward for that? We had no money; we had no health, life, or car insurance! My diabetic wife had gone without her Insulin for several weeks. I was suffering chest pain, but had decided not to let anybody know it. Sadly, in view of the fact that I'd had a heart attack before, this was foolish. Between eating a subsistence family meal and going to Emergency Room, I had chosen to put whatever meager food I could put on the table instead of going to a doctor.

Then, one day, I decided to use all my education, experience, humanity, and dignity to work and help others plan and act so they'd never have to go through this.

My thinking when I started writing this book was to determine whether this global economic mess is the fault of Democrats or Republicans. Was it the bankers that took the TARP money? Was it the Chief Executive Officers, (CEOs)? Was it a conspiracy? Before writing this book, I did not know whether any of the above was true or false. You will find my answers to the above thoughts and questions!

"Professor, why is the eBook for the Leadership and Organization Development not on the course shell?" was what I was being asked right at the moment that I was trying to find out whose fault this awful economic mess was. Unfortunately this question had to wait a few more minutes, hours, or even years before I could get my thoughts together and find the answers.

"Mr. Razban, you are one of the best Senior Management and Technology Consultants we could find. We are a half a billion hardware company and we have just acquired these software companies for more than $22,000,000. We do not understand them and they do not understand us. The executive recruiter that has given your name to us speaks very highly of you. Please sign this contract and work with us in fixing this expensive problem. Your experience at HP and National is similar to what he desperately need here too. Is the hourly fee of $90.00 per hour OK with you on a two month contract?" I was imagining or hallucinating this since I had been asked these many times before. I had a comfortable life and never worried about money. I was going on business trips all around the world flying business class and staying in four star hotels. I loved my job and almost al of my clients seemed to like and respect my work. After all I had been granted a patent that brought HP and National $55,000,000. In review after review I had been told that I was one of top 5% professionals in the consulting because I could well with people and produce outstanding results. However, the irony was that I would have happy to be a good car salesman and earn that $2,000 per month salary which was the best that I and many other consultants could do at that time of the Global Financial Crisis.

The interesting thing is that I would go back to work as a professor and as a Senior Management and Technology Consultant again. Therefore, the promise of this book is that by reading this book you too can get back to work in your field too.

This book helps us understand that since there is almost no job security these days, how you can be the CEO of your own life and career; It helps us understand that these days we need to have three different careers at the same time to prevent long-term unemployment and its devastating effect; It talks about how to have our main careers, and secondary careers on the standby, and also how to even survive serious economic downturns by having a desperation job possibility too.

Have you thought about what you want to have in your career as well as your life some thirty years later as you look back at things? In fact this book helps you to "go back to the future" to determine what is important to you now and thirty years later as if thirty years later was today. This has helped many people immensely in planning their careers and lives.

Waiting for customers in that dealership, I wanted to have a job real bad; I wanted to be productive; I wanted to be happy with my life and my job. Who does not want any or all of these? I bet you, too, want the same things. The fact remains that people in that dealership were really nice to me and I had no complaints. I was proud of earning that $2,000 per months from them as it was hard work and made me cherish that paycheck even more than other fat paychecks that I was used to getting. Right at that moment the choice was between going unemployed and this job.

Many people chose to go unemployed rather than take a job like this. However, the most important thing is that you and I still need to earn a living and put bread on the table. The question expands to how we can do this in this time of economic uncertainty. How will I be able to work during these turbulent market days?

The above question kept lingering in my mind. While I was proud of working and rejoiced in the low income that I had, I was also daydreaming about how I can get those executive or prestigious jobs that I used to have again. As a self-made person I had work extremely hard to become a top notch senior consultant who was greatly respected and appreciated and recognized as a mover and shaker who was a miracle worker. I was elated any time I saw my team happened to be happier and more productive than other teams in the company. I missed all the great things that came with being a high-level management consultant.

However, please do not take me wrong. I think that any job in this world has a great deal of dignity. This dignity is even bigger when one is helping the humanity. I felt this dignity even in my first job that was working in Jet Propulsion Laboratory at the University of Wisconsin-Madison helping researchers. In 1968, the minimum wage was $1.50 an hour. Since I was working 15 hours a week my gross income was $$22.50 each week. I never forget that right after I got my first paycheck I went to one of the clothing stores in campus and bought an "H.I.S." shirt. I had seen a few other students had a similar shirt that looked great on them. So, I had to treat myself to this too and it was a big deal. That shirt, those days cost $7.00. Later on I would buy Nordstrom suites that would cost $1,000.00 or get tailor made shoes for $200.00 from Hong Kong. But nothing felt as good as that $7.00 shirt in 1968 that I had paid from the very hard work that I had done.

However, it is very important to note that following the same ideas that are presented here in this book, I was able to apply the concept of triple-decker bus to my own career. This meant that I will continue to have what is my primary career as a senior consultant. However, it also meant that I created the standby and desperation careers as well just to not go without a job for any extended amount of time.

My primary career eventually got me a fantast consulting contract reporting to CEO of a $500 million dollar company.

My standby career ended up being an educator and an author serving as a visiting professor in an outstanding career-oriented university.

My desperation job is now torturing Math and Sciences as well as preparing college-bound students for their SAT or GMAT entrance exams.

This book helps you, in a step-by-step fashion, to build a better career for yourself, your community, country, and the world. The ideas presented here enabled and inspired many, including me.

Please Contact: bruce@razban.com

CHAPTER 1
Global Financial Crisis, Layoffs, and Job Insecurity

In order to give you those step-by-step ways of building job security for you, let me explain how our country got very close to a 1929 style recession in 2008.

While I was writing my first book, *Layoffs and Hope*, and when Wall Street lost 400 or more points in one day in 2008, I wrote about the financial devastation that could follow. In a heated discussion with a radio host at the Stanford University Student Radio Station, he had warned me about the death of American Capitalism as we knew it. What was eerily ironic about this discussion was that it was taking place in the basement of Memorial Building, right across the narrow street separating Stanford Business School, the Mecca of American capitalism, and this campus radio station.

Having gone through the dot-net bubble bust and many other periods in Silicon Valley when jobs were almost impossible to find, I finally succeeded in finding a job at Toyota Sunnyvale as an Internet Sales Manager. I was delighted to get this job!

As a frightened sixty year old American professional trying to sell cars, I had to quietly admit to myself that American Capitalism might have had an untimely death, destroying my financial future, life, and my country. It must have happened whether I liked it or not! Along with this death, my career had also died a miserable death.

Going through the grief process of losing job after job, I scorned myself for not having listened to my career coaches. My career coach, and later on my best friend for life, Jerry Weiner, had warned me early in my management career that, "Bruce, there is no such a thing as job security! It is granted that companies are trying their best to help us rest assured that the company cares for us and fights for our job security, but they cannot do it. We have to do it for ourselves! Even if they could, we cannot trust our livelihood to someone else! We cannot do this, no matter how good they are and how much they care!"

For a decade or so, when the job market was hot, I chose not to totally listen to his advice. Jerry Wiener was a graduate of the GE School of Management, and he knew what he was talking about. My first career coach, Jim Otts, with extensive management experience from Hewlett-Packard, one of the most respected companies, had echoed similar things.

After all, I was an Honors graduate of the University of Wisconsin - Madison, with an MS degree, who had worked on postgraduate studies for another four years there. I had had some of the best continuing education possible in seminars and classes offered by Stanford University Business School and their technical courses, for years. Therefore, I was highly marketable, or at least I thought so.

I had been a director, and later a senior management and technology consultant who was one of the best of the best. So, I reasoned that I should be highly marketable.

Wrong, wrong, wrong!

I ended up being more than two years without a job, receiving repeated warnings from the Bank of America regarding the foreclosure of my house. Bank of America was my business partner over the years; it was my ambition to someday be the CEO of the Bank of America. It took a bankruptcy declaration some 12 hours before my house was to be auctioned that stopped the foreclosure action for a short while. Right about that time, in an NPR radio broadcast, someone was saying that we have become a nation of vultures, referring to bankruptcies. I had too much trust in America to accept this.

I was not going to take this lightly, this time, where the entire world seemed to be unemployed. I decided that as a senior management and technology consultant with about thirty years of experience, I owed it to others to share my experience to inspire, and empower others. There were two other things too:

- First, I had served the White House as a Silicon Valley community leader in the job creation activity back in 2010. I and my best colleagues and friends decided that we must share our learning and propose a solution.
- The second thing was that I had personally lived this life of unemployment. Thus, I was optimistic that I could inspire and empower other people.

This solution manifested in two parts. The first part was that we saw it absolutely necessary to explain what was happening with the world economy, and encourage others to plan and manage their careers and jobs. In addition to this, I had been a volunteer helping those who were fired or were victims of a layoff get back on their feet, and even thrive, during my thirty years of experience.

Thus we "bottled" all this information in step by step

solutions and presented it in this book.

We created www.jobsjobsjobsjobs.com in addition to my consulting website, www.razban.com as a live, interactive, and proactive website to help those who needed help.

Let me put things in perspective. Right about middle of 2008, when Wall Street tumbled and crashed more than 400 points in one day, a massive tsunami-grade revolution had taken place.

The Re-invented American Global Capitalism (RAGC) was experiencing an invisible, earth-shattering, and painful birth.

What had worked before in the business and American worlds would no longer work! We had to learn and practice a new world economic and business order. What we usually did as the members of the government, as business persons, and especially banks, would not work anymore.

The dimensions of this change were colossal. One day it seemed like the old tested and tried steam engine technology that had served us so well was working. In an earthshaking way, the next day, it became clear that the old ways were not a way to run a railroad anymore, or the global economy would collapse, as it nearly did in 2008. We had been catapulted from our previous steam engine mentality and speeds to supersonic global, Internet, and intellectual capital hurried and horrible life over night. What is worse is that we were sleep at the switch.

It became obvious that we were now in the supersonic intergalactic business, and we had to reform to comply with this massive revolution.

The supersonic intergalactic is exactly what the CEO of Virgin Atlantic, Richard Branson had accomplished. He is a champion of thinking outside the box, and thus making things happen. With Virgin Atlantic, he created a successful airline when ever since the 1920s the airline business had been one of the most difficult ones. Profit margins got less and less as the price of a barrel of oil skyrocketed, yet he succeeded. In my book he is a major hero!

Just like him, we, too, can be heroes. Fortunately, being a hero in this time is a lot easier than trying to survive on an unemployment benefits check or attempt to chase that illusive job security related to a paycheck!

Imagine that, you are the CEO of Boeing. Then think that one day, all financial analysts and so-called crystal ball experts were hitting your beloved company in news media! What would you do?

Let me tell you what Boeing did. Their smart management realized that what had worked before did not work anymore. They had to think out of the box and take some risks. This was exactly what they did. Their management bet almost the entire company on the design and manufacturing of the first Jumbo Jet, the Boeing 747. They did this in spite of scary predictions from news media and business and economy experts. It paid off handsomely.

As Alvin Toffler had predicted in his book, "Future Shock", published in 1960s, the only constant from then on would be change!

It's ironic that a few years ago, Boeing had to bet the farm again. This was the invention of Boeing 787, the DreamLiner. The Boeing 787 uses composite materials for the fuselage and has a "bent" wing structure that results in much smoother flight and fifteen to twenty percent better fuel economies!

In the spirit of Virgin Atlantic and Boeing, let's start by taking our first heroic and out of the box step! To prepare, we will ask you to think of all the jobs you've had. If you cannot remember all of them, let's start with a few. Just make a list!

To help you, we have provided the following area to write in:

My Jobs:

1.   High School and College:
    a.   ---
    b.   ---
    c.   ---
2.   First Job:
3.   Present Job:
4.   Other jobs in between:
    a.   ---
    b.   ---
    c.   ---

Jobs List Number 1.

Congratulations! A Chinese proverb says "A journey of thousand miles starts with a single step!" You have every right to be proud of your accomplishment so far. By doing this, you've taken matters in your own hands. Your frustrations and anxiety about unemployment, underemployment, and unhappy employment will now start to diminish. Your self-confidence in your ability to be the CEO of your life and career has now redoubled. You might consider a fifteen minute break, just taking a walk or drinking a cup of coffee or tea to celebrate this first success.

Now, after that celebration, let's use List number 1 to build our Table Number 1. We are here to help you. By the way, I, too, decided to take some time off and relax. Public TV stations in San Francisco area broadcast Charlie Rose's program around 12:00 Midnight. One night, a somewhat tired Charlie Rose was politely asking questions from two financial experts about the recent collapse of the stock markets. Then in a way quite untypical of Charlie, he asked the next question that I am sure he knew was boring, only to get some boring answer!

Then as if he had come back to life, Charlie introduced his next guest, Chef/Restaurateur David Bouley. David appeared to be a well-tanned, confident, and successful person in his job, beaming a wide contagious smile. "David, it was twenty years ago when you were in my program last. What have you been doing with yourself?" was Charlie's question.

"Oh, I have been very busy expanding my business and opening new restaurants!" David's answer came as a fresh breath of air to the program. One look and I was convinced that David was telling the truth and that I could trust him. Remember that trust and loyalty thing that is critical in business success? David proudly added that he had been to Tokyo and other places, and his business was thriving because he was providing healthy and tasty food. What he was saying was that he had mutual trust and loyalty with customers and employees. He added that he is following the same thing, and he seemed to be full of energy and exuberance. "Charlie, one more thing, we are teaching and learning a different cooking methodology to someday offer specially prepared, nutritionally balanced, and tasty food for our customers."

Charlie Rose's guest had gained my respect, and my promise that I will dine in one of his restaurants, since he was offering a value-added solution for many of us.

David is an example of what the jobs of future will be like. He indeed was the CEO of his work and his life! The future success will be for those who work for themselves and are super-specialized in one or several marketable, certifiable, and value-add niches; they have a following in the form of customers with trust and loyalty; they keep being customer-centered, and they are always in tune with the customer's values and desires.

In *Too Big to Fail* book, the title says everything. Management and customers thought that the bigger the company was, the safer it would be, and it will provide better service. In the second half of 2011 we are seeing that this false. In *Layoffs and Hope* I predicted that some of these big corporations are just like dinosaurs. Their massive size creates inefficiencies that eventually spell their demise. Bank of America shares have fallen to $7.20 in late August 2011. As much as some people hate Bank of America, I have developed a strong business relationship with many of their employees over the thirty years that I have been their customer.

Let me also introduce another thing at this point. Mr. Bolles' book series have helped job seekers for more than a decade. They have been helping me and many others in finding a job and managing our careers. His latest *"What Color is Your Parachute?"* Also indicates that if you are not as excited about your job, or cannot find any in your line of business; it's time to change careers. Richard Bolles is author of some of the most powerful job and career books. He is affectionately known as "Mr. B" among his disciples, such as me.

In a program on National Public Radio, there was s discussion of employees bolting out of companies for the following reasons in these turbulent financial times:

1. They are tired of the toxic work environment that forces them to act like a zombie without any job security,
2. As painful as being unemployed might be, those who have these death march jobs are getting to a point that they are telling themselves that no job is worth dying for.
3. They are flocking to teaching and nonprofits, just to do something good for their community. Remember that when we say no to money, we get a serenity and peace of mind that no amount of money can buy!

This happened to me and my best friend and trusted colleague, Mr. Mark Fairbanks. We had each gone to more than fifty interviews without finding a job. At the beginning, we soon had learned that by writing books and composing music we can serve our community.

The reward for this effort was huge. By allocating two

hours each night to my writing, I was doing what was my passion. In the process of helping others, I had a great deal of peace and serenity during those two hours that I was doing something creative that I believed in it. Mark took his guitar with him while driving to some God-awful job interview, and came back with first pass lyrics and music composition for a future CD to help inspire the jobless. This made the difficult task of going to an interview a bit more palatable.

This is powerful. When I write, I'm in a trance. The two hours and some 2,000 or so words seem to go effortlessly from my mind and heart to the computer screen. This is a healing process which was recommended by my therapist.

As I mentioned, for more than thirty years, I have tried to help those who are unemployed as a volunteer. Please do not get me wrong; I have no jobs or any money to give. However, I can be a good listener and a good person to sometimes suggest some ideas based on my own experience in the roller coaster of the consulting job market.

Listening to a single mother of two who was unemployed just as long as I'd been, I realized the same routine. She was blaming herself for letting the job go. She was convinced that her laziness was the cause. Then with tears in her eyes, she said that she had to give up the kid's custody so they can have a roof over their heads and eat some food. She was not able to provide any of that. She had totally internalized it all.

However the truth is that in these turbulent times, we will see more and more of these things. Most important, we have to realize that these are not our fault.

In *Do What You Love and Money Will Follow*, there is a strong idea that one has to be true to herself and do what she loves rather than being the prisoner of a paycheck in a dead-end job. Now, as for me, I've done what she has recommended. I've done what I love in writing books to help others. The money has not exactly followed, yet. However, I do have confidence that someday that will change.

May I ask you question number 1?
What job or profession is your love or passion?
How can you love and be there for your loved ones at the same time while you are working?
What job or career maximizes the above?
Please feel free to jot down whatever comes to your mind for the

above question at this juncture. Your answer does not have to be complete at this point. It might just be OK to skip this or any other questions that we might ask you. However, please continue reading, and some time later you might want to go back to the question and answer it.

A former NSC executive told me that for the most of his career he worked extremely hard so as to someday make his loved ones financially secure and happy. After decades of this, he realized that he had lost the golden opportunity to be with and love his wife and children.

Please do not forget that our country suffered a devastating financial crisis in 2008. This American crisis permeated around the world, causing the Global Financial Crisis. Our banking system almost collapsed. Many people lost their jobs, and even their homes. Unfortunately, in some cases, they even lost their faith in the American dream all together.

The most powerful superpower of the time, the United States of America, was brought to its knees economically.

Sadly, many CEOs who were put on pedestals and worshiped and respected as titans of Capitalism, found themselves as accused perpetrators and villains for this crisis.

Images like that of Bernie Madoff going to jail in handcuffs poisoned the trust and respect that was freely and to some extent lovingly had been given to bigger-than-life CEOs.

Then there were senate hearings where Goldman Sac's executives, previously known as the golden boys of the gold-standard company, stood seemingly like the accused in the congressional hearings.

What has happened to the American CEOs who used to move mountains?

As unprecedented double digit unemployment figures ignited near-revolt conditions for the American middle class, cries of "American capitalism is dead!" echoed in the media. We had surely arrived at a near economic depression like that of the 1920s!

`   Frequent and massive layoffs, and revolving door "At will" hire-fire corporate practices created rampant "Fear of Sudden Job Loss" among the majority of employees. The resulting workplace toxicity stifled American inventiveness and created havoc, destroying any remaining job satisfaction or security that employees felt they deserved.

The mutual trust and loyalty which was cornerstone of the

American workplace prowess had substantially diminished. Jobs and creativity, which was the success engine behind the American economy, had burned to the ground. Without mutual trust and loyalty, American industry produced lower quality products. This reduced the profits that massive and frequent layoffs were supposed to improve.

A CBS 60-Minutes TV program report concluded that Americans were workaholics who were generally unhappy with their work.

Skyrocketing layoffs, home foreclosures, and bitter divisions in American politics, induced by financial crisis, resulted in next-generation Americans being less affluent than the previous generation; the first time this had happened to generations of Americans.

Finger-pointing and saber-rattling in putting shame and blame on others saturated American news media.

California, the Golden State, was nearly bankrupt!

My first book, *Layoffs & Hope: Advice and Inspiration for Better Work Life* was published in March of 2009, clearly predicting and explaining that layoffs were the root cause. About six months later, the cover of *Time* magazine had discovered what I had many years ago; that layoffs do not work in the long run. *Newsweek*, nine months after my book was published, arrived at exactly same conclusion that had been made in my book, heralding that layoffs are destructive and they cannot work in the long term. More emphatically, the entire nature of work on a global basis had changed drastically and forever. The work that our folks knew might never be there again for us.

Nevertheless, the fact remained that I was highly marketable and I had successfully navigated tough markets before. Even with this fact, I had not found anything. I had sent many resumes and had gone to many interviews. However, it seemed like nobody was hiring. Of course, Age Discrimination was a factor since I was over 60. Yet, my excellent background and solid connections had to find me a job as they had always done. "Professor, do you want me to sign this paper?" was what I was being asked while I was drowned in self-pity and rage about having had to sell cars as a desperation job in spite all my senior management and technology consulting experience. The honest truth is that I seemed to rejoice in having a job. Any job was fine. In fact, I would have been happy with selling cars if I was really good at it. Somehow, my gut feel seemed to stubbornly put me on notice that I was not that much of a good car salesman. "Sorry, professor, do I sign here?" was being asked again and this time I had to answer it.

Layoffs & Hope, in an uplifting way, had tried to offer alternatives to layoffs. The most important aspect of the book was to show how we can cope and recover in almost impossible economic conditions.

For example, one of the final chapters of this book says that America needs to do what America is expected to do by the rest of the world. This is to lead! However, little did I know at that time that America would arrive at a crossroads that requires it to chose between being a third-world country or being the ultra-power that the rest of the world wants America to be.

Remember that:
- The Nazis could not destroy us, or force us to stop being a symbol of freedom for the world,
- Pearl Harbor did not succeed,
- The 911 terrorist acts could not destroy us.

The hell of it, right at the time of this writing, is that we, as Americans, do not like to see ourselves as losers. The world does not need to see us as the losers, either. However, right now, we and many other world citizens do see us as losers.

America will triumphantly rise up again and lead the world to a freedom and business economy that the digital revolution requires, and supposedly empowers and enables us to do. We will show you how America and you and I can cope, heal, and then thrive, even in this economy and in these turbulent years!

You will read about things such as Click University, Marketable and Certifiable skill set, and being CEO of your own company and life that will empower and inspire you to achieve the greatest potential that you and your career are capable of.

Remember that people and companies do not fail; they just fail to plan and then execute on their action plans!

Are we doomed to fail? Hell no! We will thrive!

Please Contact: bruce@razban.com

CHAPTER 2
Brief Summary of American Work Life and Management

Up until about a hundred years ago, company owners were also managers. They did everything that was needed to commercially operate a company and produce profits.
Since this was their company, they cared and did the best they could. In addition, they had ultimate power.

Management, as we know it now, is somewhat of a new concept. Two things made it mandatory to hire outsiders as employees to manage the operation of a company to make profits. In other words, bring some outsiders to work not with his or her money, but to work with other people's money. The two factors are these:

- The owners realized that management is a discipline all by itself, and they needed professionals to do the management part,

- As companies grew, the owners could not possibly do everything, and they hired accounting, book keeping, and foremen to run the operation.

- This concept of being a manager and working with "Other People's Money, i.e. OPM was invented. OPM turned out to be as addictive as Opium!

Then it became necessary to have one focal point of contact; to have one person who was responsible for everything. This gave birth to the CEO concept.

The CEO was to be the person who was in charge of everything and responsible for everything. Also, there was a Board of Directors to assist her. This is the rule, and they have to do the job. If they do a great job, they deserve that skyrocketing salary. But, if they fail and lose jobs by the thousands, then they have failed and they need not be promoted or get those extremely high salaries. In *Layoffs and Hope*, I had recommended a CEO Accountability Act, CEOAA. This was similar to MDs having their own professional policing and enforcement of principles.

May I now ask you question number 2?
Question: What are your hobbies? How much time do you spend on them each week, for example?

Would it not be nice if your play and work became one and the same for you? Would it not be nice if you only worked four hours a week and made a great income? There is a book on this topic that claims that contrary to our American workaholic attitudes these days, it is possible to work only four hours a week and yet make a lot of money. Another book is titled, *Do What you Like and Money Will follow!*

My experience with many corporations and their C-Level executives and CEOs was that the majority of them was pre-occupied with making the company look good in the iron-fisted Wall Street "Two Quarters Profit or Die" at any price.

It also seemed to me that they were obsessed with the steam engine management mentality that made massive and frequent layoffs, product and service minimization just to appease Wall Street even if it destroyed company and many people's careers in the process.

However, in spite all these grim look, there were High Performance Companies (HPOs) who seemed to succeed not only under the difficulties mentioned above, but they succeeded when many other companies could not.

One of those companies is HP. I had the pleasure of working for them directly or as a consultant for many years. One reason HP was such a big success was the HP Way that encouraged teamwork, consensus, and respect for all employees and customers.

I am sure that you have heard the saying that when the student is ready, the teacher will show up. This is what happened to me. I had carefully studied HP school of management and also I was lucky to work for several HP managers. But what was very interesting was that I got a chance to talk to both Mr. Hewlett and Packard on several occasions. One of those occasions was when I met both of them during a book signing at Stanford University Bookstore.

They both told me that HP success was based on the fact that each individual employee and each individual customer was respected and treated as nicely as possible. In their minds a company or an organization was just as good as people who worked there or run the organization. As such there had to be trust and there has to be a big tendency to do the best that is possible.

Unfortunately, HP also fell victim to some of the same scandals and mismanagement that had caused trouble for many companies after 2005. Yet, with all this, HP of the previous years was universally respected as the royalty of companies.

Also, as I mentioned, HP was indeed my best employer during my 32 years or so of experience. I never forget that I could not wait to go to work in the morning and the work environment was so friendly and productive that I have missed that all the time I was working for other companies. I did have a happy work and a happier life since the work was going so well.

So, it might be a good idea for us to find those better jobs by applying what I have to say in this book. Also, this will help to make ourselves more and more needed by companies. In fact, by making sure that we have the marketable, certifiable skill set we can increase our chances of doing well. We can do well as an employee of a company as well as being the CEO of our own career and life.

If we constantly make sure that we are adding value to the company and our own resume, if we make sure that we are in the loop in networking, then we feel better about ourselves and do better for the company.

However, at the same time we must remember that we are talking about three careers just like a triple-decker bus. In fact, we are saying that in the future, we must have three careers instead of just one. The success in the future is to have three careers in one. We used the concept of the triple-decker bus to give you a vision, a mental picture of how things will look like. What this points out is that most successful people in their careers or even personal lives have had to attack the career life in a three prong attack since one was just not enough. Please look at the picture of this triple-decker bus at the bottom of each chapter and a smaller picture near each important point. The first floor in this triple-decker bus is our main career, the second is the standby, and finally the third is the desperation jobs.

For example, my primary career and the first floor on my career bus, is that I am a senior management and technology consultant. This is where most of my education, working career, and jobs have been in. The second and standby is being a professor. And the third is tutoring. I will use all my experience and education to help you have a happy work and life as well.

Please Contact: bruce@razban.com

CHAPTER 3
Brief Summary of American Executive Management and CEOs

Towards the end of chapter 2, there were a few questions about our hobbies. At first, this might not look like an important question. However, I assure you that it is. For example, I finally took one golf lesson from an instructor after having done my homework in making sure that he was the best they could offer. This made golf an excellent hobby for me for many years to come.

During one of those lessons, he told me that he used to be a director at one of the big semiconductor companies, and he was miserable at that job. He did not like hours and hours of sitting in semi-dark rooms, watching presentation after presentation that did not really say anything useful. Being from Wyoming, he longed for outdoors.

In the summer months, he would usually rush to his car after the end of the day and drive directly to the nearest golf course, in Sunken Gardens. He would spend the rest of the day until dark to get the exercise and clear his mind.

One day during one of those horrible Microsoft Power Point slide presentations, he decided that he'd had it, and decided to start his alternative career, teaching golf to friends and others. He would do this for free if needed, just to learn to become a good teacher. He kept his "day job," which was being a director at a major corporation.

"Bruce, I was a senior manager and dreaming of becoming an executive. I did a lot of hard work to get there. Unfortunately, that was not my cup of tea. After I had gotten enough experience and I knew that I was good as a golf instructor, I placed an ad in a local newspaper. The word got around that I was a good golf instructor and slowly I was getting more and more students. Before I knew it, it was time to retire, and I decided to do golf instruction full time. I had to learn how to use the cash register to sell things in the golf club's store. Now, I'm as happy as I have ever been in my career and life. My health has benefitted considerably as a result of the exercise I get while I teach." This was what he shared with me about his career.

In many small, medium, and large companies, becoming an executive is a difficult task. In many cases an MBA is needed, and the individual needs to learn how to navigate the politics of the company. In other words, we learn how not to rock the boat in a top-heavy corporation while producing no value-add results.

Some time ago, there used to be a foreman leading a number of workers. Then there were supervisors who were a bit more formal and still responsible for leading. These were the first line managers. They were the managers, and a number of workers reported directly to them.

After that, a totem pole effect got started. In this case, workers reported to a first line manager, and those first line managers reported to a senior manager or a director. The hierarchy got even more complex. Then the senior managers and/or directors would report to a vice president, and vice presidents would report to the CEO.

In the later part of my career, many companies decided to have a flattened organization to save money and be more agile. Unfortunately, the management layers gradually reappeared, and bureaucracy exploded again.

Some organizational developers think that having layers of management was good for the business, since it brought a structure and demanded systematic processes. Others argue that layer after layer of management does not create enough value; it loses its touch with customer reality; it generates a dangerous isolation.

Is this global economic mess the fault of Democrats or Republicans? Or was it the bankers who took the TARP money and ran? Or was it the CEOs and the huge salaries we paid to the CEOs? Or was it a conspiracy? I do know that I have not answered these questions yet. However, let me point out at this point that you will be surprised to find out who the real culprit(s) are, later on.

It's important to note that I respect American executives, and I do know that most of them are dedicated and extremely motivated. This book does not advocate that you, as a successful C-level executive, should give up your hard-earned job, resign, and go into hiding. At least not yet!

However, as you will see in the triple-decker bus concept of careers and jobs, the book does advocate that even a C-level executive is not immune from job insecurity, and they, too, need to be ready if a sudden job loss happens.

Question number 3:

Suppose that you won a huge amount of money in some kind of legal lotto, or what the heck, even semi-legal ones.

Typically, people spend the first few months getting used to idea of having a lot of money. They tend to do some of the fun things that they always wanted to do but did not have time and/or money.

Suppose that you had all the fun that you always wanted to have and could not afford. After that great time, now you have to continue some sort of life. What would you be doing? This will be a great clue in helping you decide what your career should be, even if you are not a lottery winner.

Just to fortify this; think about your hobbies. This might give you another clue about what it is that you like to do.

In addition to all these, you must take into account that your primary career must be your expertise in something that is:

- Marketable, that is, something that there is a need for it,
- Certifiable, that is something that you can get some sort of industry respected certification for,
- You are willing to be the CEO of your career and life by:
  - ✓ Empowering yourself,
  - ✓ Marketing and selling your company or expertise at all times, and
  - ✓ Doing what you like and are good at!

Following the ideas presented above, you now have left the steam engine train mentality and joined the win-win and successful job and career strategy that includes:

- Multiple choice and diversified careers and jobs at your command,
- Incorporation Liberation,
- Life and work inspiration and empowerment by being your own CEO. This means you are in charge of your career and life.

Please Contact: bruce@razban.com

CHAPTER 4
Management Crisis and Work Place Toxicity

I used to tell my friends and colleagues about my best job ever, which was at HP before the Global Financial Crisis. Usually their reaction was that they hoped that someday their company would become as good as HP was those days.

HP was so good, and their employees were so well trained, confident, and effective, that seldom anybody left HP. Many of my former HP executives, affectionately known as HPers, have nothing but good things to say about HP in those days. They would even affectionately refer to HP as "Mother HP," since it cared so much for its employees and customers.

HP-Way was such that during the first fifty years of their existence, there were no layoffs! This was because HP practiced respect for individual employees, greatly practiced teamwork, and promoted from within. This built a great deal of mutual trust and loyalty that made HP products and services superior to competition. Not only that, it created an environment of creativity resulting in outstanding innovations. In fact, for many years, HP's logo was "Re-Invent!" What little did I know that someday Capitalism needs to re-invent itself to thrive after the Global Financial Crisis.

When I was working for HP as a senior consultant in Cupertino in 1999, I did in fact have the highest level of job satisfaction. Each day, I could not wait to go to work. Each day, I was learning something new. Each day, I would enjoy the two coffee breaks with colleagues. Several of those colleagues became life-time friends. We shared vacation memories, discussed political developments, and even helped each other, in private, with personal problems.

The teamwork was so strong that when I had made a mistake, several colleagues and my manager and his manager were there to help fix it. It was not important whose fault it was. According to the HP Way, we were in this together and let's find a solution by co-operation, teamwork, and consensus.

The problem was solved fast and properly. Then we all went to have a longer than usual coffee break. I could not believe this! It seemed like the entire team was celebrating. My manager told me quietly, "Bruce, we're happy that you made this so-called mistake! We're happy that it happened before the product was shipped, and we're happy since our documentation and process flow will prevent something like this happening again!" His kind and sincere words assured me that I was not going to be fired. They were smart. They were building relationships! They had cultivated a great deal of mutual trust and loyalty in me and the team, right there and then. They did this for me, even though I was an outside independent consultant.

Two weekends later, while playing golf with another HPer, I did one of the things that HP encouraged us to do. I asked a "What if" question. Before I could dismiss it as a dumb idea, my HP friend told me, "Let's take a minute and write this down! Can we do this? I want to make sure that I do not miss anything. Bruce you're on to something." We wrote it down, and in another week we realized that we had added an excellent feature to an HP product. The mutual trust and loyalty had worked its magic even during our time off.

This feature gave us all a great deal of pride and job satisfaction. It also was a win-win situation that had resulted from teamwork, job security, and job satisfaction, which these days are extremely hard to find, and was the foundation that triggered the innovation and caring that produced this humongous success.

This fact is even clear to Hollywood. In *Airport 1975*, Joe Petroni, played by George Kennedy, is TWA's expert employee. As one of the heroes in this movie as well as others, the film clearly shows how confident he is and because of job security he is able to make all those difficult decisions to save the lives of 120 passengers on a Boeing 747. In this movie, even a child knows that 747 "Is the best aircraft ever made." This refers to superiority of American products. You will see that Boeing had to gamble almost the entire company in the reinvention of itself and its products to make the hugely successful airplane.

It's sadly ironic that management eventually, by introducing layoffs, devastated mutual trust and loyalty, ignored flight attendants' seniority, and this created an inferior ability for TWA to successfully compete. Then, a heartbreak for aviation enthusiasts like me, TWA was sold as if it was scrap metal.

Another example is Toyota and Lexus. As a Toyota employee, I had to learn the company history and its culture. In those mandatory lessons, I learned that it was a Mr. Toyoda who started the company. My family had purchased as many as eight Toyotas, and I had also purchased an ES250 Lexus. I must say that this car, which now has over 212,000 miles on it, "talks" to me. It says, "Those who built this car were happy with their jobs, and they made sure that this product is as perfect as perfect can be!" Unfortunately when Toyota started to lay off employees, those layoffs broke the mutual trust and loyalty, resulting in repeated "recalls." Toyota seldom had this kind of problem before its layoffs. To prove this point, all I have to do is point to the timing of Toyota having had to recall cars for one problem or the other after it decided to lay off employees.

Today, it is opposite!

"But Mr. Razban, are you telling me that nobody should ever be fired? Are you telling me that companies should not lay off excess employees even when they are not making money? This is certainly a recipe for destruction of many companies. Or, are you telling me that government has to make so many employee-centric rules and regulations as to make business impossible?"

My response is that if an employee, including the CEO, is not doing a good job, he has to be fired, subject to a fair verbal and written warning. In the movie *Up in the Air* which has mind-boggling resemblances with what I had discussed in *Layoffs and Hope*, George Clooney says, "I'm here to do what the company managers do not have the balls to do, and that is to lay off their employees!" The movie seems to say layoffs are OK, and in fact this team of managers goes from one company to another to do the "bloody" act of layoffs, up until a woman takes her life. Then the movie effectively turns its plot around and even some of the management resigns or decide to go do other things.

I know of three colleagues who took their own lives after they were let go from their jobs. A sudden job loss starts a sliding scale towards financial, emotional, and even health devastation.

The workplace has become such an awful thing that people are nervous. Frequent and massive layoffs; massive off-shoring; politics; dysfunctionality; fear of sudden job loss, untrustworthy colleagues; back-stabbings; firings; stress; being dangerously overworked; not being respected or appreciated; burn-outs, and even suicides; pay cuts; mandatory furloughs; impossible demands for results, and hard work are all contributing to an extremely high levels of job dissatisfaction.

In survey after survey, it becomes clear that more than

sixty percent of employees are unhappy. This unhappiness strongly manifests itself in inferior products and services. In August of 2011, a full 25% of Americans were unemployed or underemployed.

As a senior management and technology consultant working in Cisco, Kaiser Permanente, PayPal, and eBay, I quickly learned that sixty percent of daily effort went into other things than direct value-add activities.

Before I get angry calls from these companies, let me explain my thoughts on this. Kaiser Permanente was pioneered by Mr. Kaiser, who had seen a dire need for California gold seekers to get medical attention and badly needed supplies while doing the arduous task of gold mining. If you go to Oakland, on the top floor of one the buildings belonging to Kaiser, there is an attention-grabbing picture that shows Mr. Kaiser distributing crutches to children. He had seen a need for crutches for kids and, as a philanthropist, he was distributing them. He can be seen in a picture proudly giving crutches to a bunch of happy and smiling kids.

The founder of Kaiser had discovered a need, and he was directly filling that need in a value-added way. Now, Kaiser is one of the biggest health providers, and layer upon layer of management and a huge marketing and sales department has created so much more structure than was there when Mr. Kaiser was directly doing what was really needed.

For example, I have often thought about one need. This is to prepare affordable Prom dresses for high school graduates who are on a tight budget. I'll bet that you, too, can see many needs in your community, on Internet, and even among friends and colleagues that you can fulfill.

Let's take a few minutes and write down a list of these potential needs within your reach. Let us give this a try. Shall we?

Potential Needs List:

1. Needs you have
2. Needs your family has
3. Needs your friends have
4. Needs you see in the community
5. Needs in America
6. Needs in the globe

For now, we make this list without judging the items to see if they are valid or not, or whether we can make money or not. Let's use our creativity and make this list as complete as it can be.

This chapter was focused on the present management crisis that has manifested itself in work place toxicity. This is the six sigma root cause of the problem. However, we do not want to waste our time, life, and energies in the problem domain. I remember that there was a saying during the Vietnam War protest that said, "If you are not a part of the solution, you are a part of the problem!" In fact, this saying had been fully integrated in HP management culture that was:

- It is important to find what the problem is,
- Problem is defined and without blaming or judgment,
- Consider that we are all in this together; we are a team,
- As a team, we can come up with a win-win solution by using consensus by strengthening agreements common cooperation,
- Finally get agreement and start on working on a solution.

Never the less as a senior management and technology consultant, I am positive that instead of being angry at each other and creating war between us and them, we must regroup and do a great deal of teamwork to solve problems.

As a Visiting Professor at Keller Graduate School of Management in DeVry University, teaching the HR876 course to MBA students I made a discovery myself. Teaching this course that was about management of change, it became obvious that to manage a change from a problem to a solution requires that we first have an image of how things are now and the mental image of how things should be in the future.

As you are reading this book, I am sure that you too are thinking about changing your career and/or your life as well. So, try to put your vision together. Be ready to tell yourself that you can and will be having a better career. It is important that in your mind's eye you see yourself as succeeding in this future that is depicted in the vision.

To achieve that vision, you need to demonstrate leadership. In business, leaders have to have a message that they can communicate well to the others; also leaders must not be averse to taking calculated risks; true leaders are not scared of losing sometimes. However, they always try and try again until they succeed. Leaders must have followers. In our case these followers and supporters are our family, colleagues, and friends.

I mentioned communication above. The important thing to note is that communication is not just transferring information from one person to another. The real communication is to get the other person to buy in your vision and your ideals.

Many good leaders are respected and liked by their followers because their message is a message of hope and inspiration and good leaders manage to liberate others from a dysfunctional situation.

For example, Dr. Mohandas Mahatma Gandhi liberated India from British colonization. Without his leadership, India might be the biggest democracy in the world.

In this case we are saying that you will lead yourself into the vision of being liberated as the CEO of your own career and life. Go ahead and start that startup that you have always dreamed of starting. Go ahead and go back to school if you miss certain skills. You can not not succeed.

When I was chosen to be the faculty speaker in a graduation ceremony at Keller Graduate School of Management, I ended up my speech by saying that we should never, ever give up five minutes before the real miracle to happen.

The fundamental components of the problem are that the old Capitalism is dead. The new reinvented American Global Capitalism (AGC) is based in integration of Internet and human intellectual capital to the old materials based Capitalism that imploded with destructive greed manifesting itself in take the money and run operative process.

Please Contact: bruce@razban.com

CHAPTER 5
Work Place of the Future

While there is a more detailed chapter on this later on in this book, we'd like to point out some basic and fundamental ideas.

Human beings have the same needs they had when they lived in a cave. As Maslow determined, there is a hierarchy of needs that have to be met. We need food, we need shelter, we need our social interactions, etc.

When I was working at Plantronics in Santa Cruz, I had most of my work-related needs met. I was learning new things each day. I was feeling needed, since without me they could not release their products. I worked for Jim Otts, who was an HPer and an excellent manager.

He was such outstanding manager, who one day during his "Management by Walking Around," which is typical at HP, he had figured out that, that day I was not quite myself.

He asked, "Bruce are you OK?"

"Jim, I'm OK, but I have some outside problems. I'm trying to be professional and do my job. So, let outside problems belong to outside," I said, expecting him to give up and go away.

His reaction was quite the opposite, "Please do not tell me the details, but is this something I can help? Maybe, you want to take a few days off? Maybe it's something that our legal department can help you resolve? Maybe it's a girlfriend problem; in that case Dave can help you. He is a lady's man, and he knows how to solve any problems with women."

I had to respond, saying, "Jim it's none of the above. It's personal and I do not care to talk about it."

With a big smile, he said "OK, let's go to the Santa Cruz pier and do the two hour lunch! Do you mind if I bring two of your coworkers along, too?" Then he proudly added that "This is a company treat since your group has done a great job."

I'll never forget that lunch that was on a pier right on Pacific Ocean. The food was great, and although they respected my request to keep my problem private, their joking and telling stories helped me forget my dilemma, at least during those two hours.

Jim, as my manager, felt that it was his job to make sure that I was OK. He was not there to get maximum productivity from me and others and then let us go. He was building mutual trust and loyalty; he was building a working relationship that lasted for two decades and spanned several companies. His HP management training had prepared him well for this. He knew that the best way a company could make money from our work was to take good care of Plantronics employees and Plantronics customers.

Frankly, I care less how much a CEO makes. If they do the job right, they should make bundles of money. But when they do not keep in mind the human aspect, or when they keep doing layoffs like clockwork, I object to that.

They are paid to manage and lead! This is their job!

When I was working at Zilog, one of my employees had a motorcycle accident. I felt that as his manager, it was my responsibility to visit him in the hospital and cheer him up.

The workplace of the future is already beginning to show its shape. People will work more out of their homes, and this will bring more of a work/life balance. People will specialize, to a high level, in some expertise that can be certified and is marketable. Many people will have a one-person company that is incorporated and is well known for one or the other type of product or service. The company's reputation is calculated on a minute-by-minute basis, based on actual and real-time customer input that is honest and fair. The job satisfaction, productivity, and profitability of any company is calculated and displayed on the central display for everyone to see.

Peter Senge, an MIT management expert believes that high school of the future will not look like anything we have now. He says and I agree that the future of education will be to send students to the real world so they can practice what they have learned and in fact he is saying that successful business people of the future will have to be the CEOs of their careers and lives right from high school.

This totally coincides with what I as the faculty of the Keller Graduate School of Management at DeVry University told my graduating MBA students that the education of the future will be entrepreneurial, life long, and on the job learning unlike when people got a degree and they were done with their education.

In 2011 it became increasingly clear to me that in order to learn, I have to rely more on the Google and youtube.com as my latest and greatest education tools. In fact a 2 minute youtube.com clip if done properly can be as effective as 200 pages of an educational textbook.

Right about then many universities also decided to make

sure they were well represented in the Internet. Stanford University or MIT and Harvard for that matter started a systematic effort to put some of their courses, or sections of courses online. They had quickly realized the power of Internet.

In DeVry University course for managing change and leadership that our MBA students take I just cannot teach without a Stanford University clip that shows Carly Fiorina, a former HP CEO telling us that change, any change, creates fear. Then she continues by saying that unless we manage this change, we cannot successfully change.

And, going from a career of being at the mercy of others and worrying about layoffs, downsizing, and unemployment or underemployment, we will go to be the CEO. This is a big change and might just make us scared. But, remember that unless we deal with this fear, we will not be able to succeed. And this book inspires and empowers you to make the change succeed.

Considering the fact that majority of American business is conducted by small companies as they make the backbone of our technology and business, the business successful people of the future will be more like these heroes in my book that I like to show case their careers:

A powerful example is Dr. Dominick Curatola, who is a famous cardiologist in San Francisco Bay Area. I first met him when I took my father to him when he had a serious heart problem. In those days he had an office in Los Altos, CA that looked like a house so as to make patients more comfortable and at home along with a staff which was outstanding, effective, and very caring. I was immediately impressed with his strongly confident statement that he will make my father better. This was so important for us to hear that we decided to follow each and every treatment and medication offered by him. Of course we know that doctors make the worst patients. And, my father being an MD, was no exception this rule. However, my dad seemed to respect and be very comfortable with Dr. Curatola's diagnosis.

Since this was Dr. Curatola's private practice, he made sure everything was fine and he paid a seeming unending attention to everything.

Soon my father who would be critical of many doctors was referring to Dr. Curatola as the "Doctors' Doctor!" This was because there was a mutual trust and loyalty that was established early in our appointments when Doctor Curatola made sure tht he understood the patient as well as the illness.

A few years later, when my mother needed medical attention, we found the same professional yet caring attention that got quick and impressive results.

If you look at it carefully, Dr. Curatola in that practice was the CEO of his own career and life. The money spent and earned in this practice would affect him directly.

Then it was my own turn. I had a heart attack at an early age when I was working for a major car company as a Senior Technical and Management consultant.

I had noticed that he had a copy of Top Doc Magazine in his office. This really impressed me. Just having this magazine told me that he at least tried to be the best. It also turned out that he was indeed chosen as the "Top Doc" before. A copy of this certification along with others was framed and hung to his office walls.

After my test results became available, he again took time to explain to me everything. By using pictures and other explanation he had managed to patiently explain to me what the heart attack had done and how he will make sure to stabilize my heart. And, stabilize he did.

His office was extremely helpful and effective as well as everybody was considered a long-term partner.

While he had started as a small company, his practice had grown a great deal over the many years and his patients were multiplying just as a result of word of mouth advertising.

Dr. Curatola and his office were all highly proficient in use of Internet and they kept up with the latest technology almost on a daily basis. This in fact gave them a great deal of empowerment. In addition, it was clear that Dr. Curatola, as well others in his practice, were highly aware of intellectual capital in their business. This meant constant teaching and learning from youtube.com and other sources in addition to medical seminars and Doctor Curatola conducting seminars himself. A case in point is that Dr. Curatola was one of the first professionals to use Dragon software as his dictating tool during patient visits to record and update patient files as well as order medications as accurately as possible. In addition, his office is one the few that I know is using patient portal technology so patients can update their status and input that information directly into the computer.

However, you might ask "But how about Proactive Profitable Philanthropy?" This was demonstrated and practiced when during one of my visits I indicated that I did not have any health insurance as a result of the Global Financial. After stating his empathy and sympathy in a very kind way, he added, "Well, here is what we can do. I will change all your prescriptions to generics. Then you go to the labs and tell them that they should give you a cash advance discount since you will be paying cash." As if this was not enough, he added, "Look, I know it is difficult. It has been difficult for many people. Now, since you did very well in your EKG, I will waive that cost if you promise to do even better next time in keeping your blood pressure, Cholesterol and weight in check!"

Since being a cardiologist in Dr. Curatola's primary career, he keeps up with the latest in his field. This was very evident when he was giving a lecture at El Camino Hospital to sell out audience. "Did you know that 40% of all deaths in the US are caused by heart problems? This statement and the way it was expressed got the total attention of the audience.

Then instead of lecturing or talking down to the audience, he told us that his family has had a history of heart problems. This made us feel that we were not alone with our heart problems as we heard about some others in his family too. He also exhibited the same humble pride that you can see in other successful professionals. He said, "One of my patients is 95 years old and he just stopped by to show me his brand new California Drivers License."

We owe it to ourselves to constantly learn and improve our careers. This is one of the best and most important success criterions in any business. Being a graduate of Yale University, he did continue his education all the time so he can be on top of the latest and greatest.

Teaching my MBA students, I point out to them that not only we need to diversify our careers; we also need to be multi-dimensional ourselves. Dr. Curatola happens to be a wine expert as well. In almost all his patient rooms there is also a picture of grapes and wine on the wall as well.

I will share with you other show case professional who had indeed successfully acted as CEOs of their career and life in the future pages in this book.

The American Global Capitalism (AGC) has:

 Using Internet as empowerment,

 Intellectual Capital,

 Proactive Profitable Philanthropy!

 Also, empowered and inspired by having three-in-one career and being the CEO of our careers and lives.

Please Contact: bruce@razban.com

CHAPTER 6
Near Death of American Old Capitalism and Old CEO Role

Double-digit unemployment hit the American middle class hardest. It came as a shock to majority of Americans, especially middle class Americans, to suddenly discover that they were vulnerable. For the first time, middle class Americans were facing severe rates of unemployment and home foreclosure. Fears of a near economic depression of 1920s proportions destroyed almost all consumer confidence. Also, as usual, the poor were getting brutally poorer, too.

For example, middle class consumer who could not send their kids to college; a middle class consumer who suddenly had to realize that their kids would have a lower standard of living, started to recoil. This recoiling meant that American consumers did not do the spending that they used to do. Since the American economy is based on consumer spending, lack of spending can force the American economy to implode.

This resulted in the bankruptcy of many small businesses. Many major banks and corporations, whose bigness had been their defense for generations, found themselves like dinosaurs on the verge of imminent extinction.

It was the potent combination of the disastrous decline of the American middle class and small business, which are the spine of business that created a quagmire of slippery downward slopes and thunderstorms of economic vicious cycles that converted the American Dream into an American nightmare of gigantic proportions.

Whose fault was it?

In a simplistic management model, the CEO and Board of Directors of a company are the ones that have to be at fault. This is so because, by definition, a CEO is the captain of a company's ship. He or she is supposed to be in charge of everything. Therefore, the finger of blame can fairly or unfairly y point directly at the CEO!

Was it really the CEO who was completely at fault? This was a question that I faced while writing *Layoffs and Hope*. My thirty-two years of business and management experience quickly convinced me that this witch-hunt of shame and blame would not lead to any solution.

As a manager, I had learned from the HP and GE schools

of management that it was not as important to find whose fault it was. It was more urgent and vital to find out how to collectively come up with a win-win solution, via teamwork.

It was ironic that in a discussion with a college campus radio talk show host, I heard, "Bruce, maybe American Capitalism is dead!"

Normally, I have an open mind and people can tell me anything they want, but these words being uttered in complete confidence by an American middle class man proved to be mind-boggling to me.

What was worse, these words were being sledge-hammered into my aching brain by someone I respected. As if that was not painful and alarming enough, I was hearing these words just a few yards away from one of the most prestigious business schools in the world, the Stanford University Business School. Later on, I heard that the same words were echoed about the European economy in the London School of Economics, as well as at the Sorbonne University in Paris.

A dizzying barrage of subsequent sentences followed. "Bruce, let's face it. We could not have a prosperous lifestyle forever. Look, my colleagues and I are losing our houses. My son, who graduated from an excellent university, cannot find a job. He graduated six months ago, and there are no jobs. What's worse is that he owes $92,000 on his college loans that he most likely will never be able to pay." After a relatively long and worrying pause, as if he needed to catch his breath, he continued. "Bruce, I know you love this country. I know you want things to get better, as they always did. Just tell me how!"

The student loan part of his desperate and angry talk hit me between the eyes. I graduated with Honors from the University of Wisconsin – Madison in 1971, with a grand total of $2,600 that I owed. I'd paid back most of that by being a teaching assistant/lecturer, as well as summer jobs in New York City. This broke my heart. In my experience, all these times there always was some job available. Even in 1971, where the cover of *Time* or *Newsweek* showed a college graduate working in a gas station pumping gas in his graduation garb!

In the thirty years that I've been working in Silicon Valley, I'd never seen unemployment like the 12% that exists now. I'd never seen the amount of despair, hopelessness, and downright financial devastation that I see now in my own financial case and that of others.

Writing this book, which is my fourth, is heaven-sent therapy. Writing helps me forget the fact that I'm just a few weeks or months away from being homeless if the house is auctioned out in a foreclosure sale. It also helps me think that there are still good things in this world. My wife's MD, Dr. Linda, has treated her for almost no money for these two years, and given her free samples of diabetics' medication. My therapist of many years, Suzanne, has been treating me with no payment for almost the same amount of time.

However, I'm scared. I'm really scared every time I realize that we have no medical insurance, no retirement fund, and no savings.

At first, being a manager, I blamed CEOs and Boards of Directors for having done this to us. I got especially angry when I heard that Apple computers had more cash than the US government, and still was not hiring. I got irate when I heard that Cisco is in the process of a 6,500-employee layoff. I got furious when I heard that Bank of America, my favorite bank and a symbol of American business power, will lay off 35,000 employees.

How could this be? Bank of America was my folk's bank and still to this day my entire family banks with them. In a day of near-rage after I'd heard about my foreclosure, I went to the nearby branch and conducted a 1960's style sit-in, in an anti-Vietnam War fashion. The branch VP, Charles, who was also old enough to remember Vietnam and who looked and talked just like one of the comic characters in the WKRP Cincinnati show, decided not to make a big issue and instead talked to me with respect and promised to do what he could to help. Ruby, in the same branch, was extremely helpful, and had tears in her eyes when I asked her why is the Bank of America treating a "valued customer" of more than thirty years this way? Why am I being treated like a criminal? Mike, another branch manager, has extended me the same courtesy as when my business account was bringing close to $200,000 a year. Shahin, who had helped my folks carefully plan investment of their retirement funds by helping them get the best interest rates that were available, is what I think of Bank of America. Shahin and many others have been with Bank of America thirty or more years.

More importantly, they all cared and practiced mutual trust and loyalty.

I did not borrow needlessly. As a consultant, I had to borrow during lean times and pay it back when I had contracts. I did not waste money, either. I get extremely angry when Europeans, or specially Chinese tell us that we spent too much. We did not. The American economy is consumption-based, and Americans are not penny-pinchers and cheap people by culture, and as a second nature. Even any self-hating American should admit that our life-style could not be blamed for a global financial crisis.

However, we are now millions of miles from these petty arguments. Our country, and the entire globe for that matter, is in a serious crisis. We will not only survive, but we will also thrive! It's just in American DNA to bring catastrophe to a happy ending by innovation and heroics! It will be un-American if we did not do this.

The American financial meltdown in August of 2011 is simple! It is not Congress, it is not the government, and it is not the CEOs or Boards of Directors. We can hate and blame till the end of our lives, but nothing can be fixed. Instead of cursing the darkness, let's light a candle, or better yet a torch, as the symbolic torch in the hand of Statue of Liberty.

My problem, your problem, American government's problem, Europe's problem, and the globe's problem, along with Indian, Chinese, Brazilian, and others are one and the same.

The fundamental global reality is that global economies and business realities have changed. The old rules and processes do not work anymore. There are three realities in this economy:

1. Digital economy and digital humanity,
2. Human global capitalism instead of that obsolete old materials only based American capitalism.
3. America doing what America is expected to do by the globe and that is leading by consensus and leadership by example.

In an interesting discussion with a Stanford University student during my book signing at Barnes and Noble Bookstore in San Mateo, CA, I realized that there is little object to digital economy taking over the old economy and many people agree to this. However, the digital humanity is a bit more difficult to understand and apply to our everyday life realities.

Humanity, as it always has been is related to being

43

humans and being humans at its best. It is to care for other human beings and make sure that there is benefit for all in any decision and action. In fact we will soon reach a point in our economy and business to say that to make money and to make lots of money, our business and economy has to be in the philanthropic profit making. For example a diabetic medicine that would market for $300 a box might very well bring a lot more profits if it is mass marketed in Africa and Asia for $30 a box since the $300 can only have a limited market.

I came up with this idea when I was teaching my soon to be MBA graduates. In one of the graduate classes, we divide the American economy into two time sectors: Pre-global financial crisis and post-Global financial crisis. Then it seems like in both cases companies and organizations that were success were not those that created toxic work places that forced their employees to be zombies for the fear layoffs and lack job satisfaction and job security. Furthermore it became obvious that most successful companies where those that treated their employees and customers as respected human beings and tried their best to do good for the global community.

On the second point, suppose you have a trucking company. In the old American Capitalism, your wealth could be summarized have a building and twenty trucks. In the digital economy, you must consider in addition to the material only based, which are the trucks, also the fact that your digital humanity is important too. In this case, you consider how well trained your truck drivers are; how comfortable they are in using and functioning in the digital economy; and how much job and life satisfaction they have. We can measure and we can work well with all of these.

On the third point, we need to accept that America has had a unique position in the world as being a leader on the global basis. If you have any doubts about this, please remember Google, iPhone, Tweeter, and many other innovations in the world came from American technology leadership.

Also, in addition to the American technology leadership, America has also had a unique humanitarian leadership position. Many Americans as part of the Peace Corps, and other volunteers have been doing the best possible to save and enhance humanity.

This very same humanitarian concept is magnified and expanded millions of time on the global basis. Ideas such as profit sharing and employee rights etc. all were started here in America.

The human aspect of good business actually applies to many big and small companies. In a recent Sunday I was having lunch at Michaels Restaurant in Bay Shore Golf in Mountain View. As always Mr. Michaels personally was there and he recognized me. We go back to many years ago when they had a restaurant in Sunnyvale, CA and my company which was National Semiconductor would have business lunch or dinner parties. On each and every occasion, Michaels would prove to be a great choice because they treated customers and employees with outmost humanity.

On this Sunday during a cordial conversation with Mr. Michaels, he pointed to me that he treats his employees very well. He told me about the master chef who started working at Michael's right after graduating from school and he is still there; He would proudly point out that he has helped some of his employees go to college and get advanced degrees; and he points out that in his book customer have to be treated well at all times.

In a way he is talking about Mutual Trust and Loyalty that develop in companies that are well managed. When I mentioned layoffs, his reaction was that he always does his best to avoid this since the company is just like family.

As we will see later on, America has a digital binary choice to make. Either we become that third world country that our enemies would like to see happen, or we, as the free world's leaders, choose to become that globally respected ultra-power.

Please Contact: bruce@razban.com

CHAPTER 7
New Era of American Global Capitalism (AGC) and New CEO

By definition, a CEO is responsible for everything.

That definition still holds, and will continue to hold forever. However, the era of CEO doing irresponsible things is over.

Let me give you one example. S&P was the company that downgraded American credit worthiness from AAA to AA+. This nearly crashed a scared stock market. Then the president or CEO decided to step down.

For years, and in many companies, the CEO could recklessly fire or lay off anybody they wanted. They could downsize and offshore, they could acquire, sell, or buy any other company whenever they wanted.

As Americans, we would worship these CEOs with our children's 401K education fund. As Americans we never questioned anything they did, since we felt that we were inferior to these god-like fully polished and painted symbols of ultimate power.

CEOs could do anything they wanted. The company was their sand box! They could mess up royally and then go some other place with a promotion and a much bigger salary. Unfortunately, the fact remained that some of these CEOs were not well-suited to being a CEO. However, the stock holders and the stock market were blind to this.

For more that eighteen years, I either worked for HP or worked in another company that worked closely with HP. Incidentally, Carley Fiorina started at HP at more or less the same time that I started working with the HPshopping.com as a senior consultant. I personally have developed a love/hate relationship with her as an HP executive. I loved her for redirecting HP into realizing that even HP had to make money; I hated her for her purchase of Compaq, as well as her layoff of 3,500 or more employees. HP was a company that cared for their employees and customers. Layoffs and purchase of Compaq created many divisions in the company. I, for one, used all my power as a stockholder to vote against the purchase of Compaq.

I guess that Carley had fallen in love with the idea of HP being the number one PC maker in the world.

Then, in late August of 2011, there was a terse

announcement from HP that they have dropped their PC and tablet product lines.

Nowhere in these announcements was there any indication of how many people would lose their jobs; nowhere in these announcements was there any indication of convincing reasons for doing this. This was not the HP that I knew and highly respected.

Many American companies, and, for that matter, Japanese and European countries, became addicted to layoffs as a tool to make the company look better in the profit and loss statements or during the short two quarters attention span of Wall Street.

CEOs were acting as if layoffs were part of the operation. They did not bother to realize that these frequent and massive revolving door layoffs were needed due to bad management! They seemed to think that an employee of twenty or thirty years was just like a computer. Plug them in when you need them and unplug and discard them when you do not need them.

The Walgreen's pharmacy is a good example. They, as well as many other companies, hire new people, let them learn things. As soon as they are competent and able to treat customers well, there is time for getting rid of them and hiring new cheap laborers. I say this because I care for these American icons.

Dear Mr. or Madam CEO: We are here to make a long term mutual trust and loyalty relationship between the management, employees, and most important, the customer.

I'll never forget Barbara Boxer telling Carley Fiorina in an election debate, "Please have a heart! Your company has laid off 3,500 employees!" I'm glad that Barbara got elected.

Randy Shandobil, a respected San Francisco area reporter, was shoved off a news interview with eBay CEO Meg Whitman, who wanted to be elected after spending millions of her money. Randy was perceived to ask wrong questions.

What brought the Global Financial Crisis on us was mismanagement. Do not pay attention to talking heads on TV news. We managed to get into this financial crisis, and we can manage to get out of it, clean and simple. As the "Blood Sweat and Tears" group says, "What goes up must come down!"

In an informal book reading party for this book, several of my friends and colleagues were present. Before I could read the first word, a good friend asked, "Did you know that less than twenty percent of Americans trust Congress, Republicans, or

Democrats? There is no trust in banks, employers, products, or news media! What on earth am I supposed to do? My kid brother, who is 64 years old, has just lost $200,000 of his life-time IRA, and he has gone into a deep depression. He has no money, and his brothers and sister are buying groceries for him each day. This is so bad that it's bringing me down too!"

This is not supposed to happen here in the US.

Again, before I could read the first word, there was another strong objection, "I worked fourteen years for these bastards and they gave me three months worth of severance pay and told me that I had two hours to pack up and leave the premises! How dare they?" With a few minutes of hesitation, she continued, "That company has a group that watches the disgruntled employees. After all these layoffs and mistreatment of employees, there are some employees who get angry enough, and are unethical enough, to go for revenge by introducing viruses or giving away trade secrets. Why should they care for the company that does not care for them?"

This reminded me of a young graduate of an excellent school who had to give up his apartment and go back to live with his folks in a two bedroom apartment. He told me, "I do not have resentments against anybody. I just want to have an entry-level job to get started after all this hard work I did in college. I cannot find any. My mother tells me that all that college education was a total waste if I cannot find a job. The sad thing is that nobody seems to care for the unemployed."

An older laid-off defense industry employee told me, "Bruce, since we are the same age, let me tell you that I will never, ever go to work for anybody else except for myself. All that hard work, dedication was wrong." Then, with anger radiating from his tired and sad eyes, he added, "I'm starting a company of my own. I will do or die on my own. I'll never have to do the stupid political things that I was supposed to do in that huge company where 70% to 80% of the daily work was to cover up something, or to generate some stupid report, or to play some stupid game. I've had it with them. My manager was from a third-world country that treated us with intimidation, brutality, and horror, just like the totalitarian government did in their home country."

This same 60% to 80% of daily work being consumed by politics and non-value-added activity keeps coming up in relationship to big companies. This supports what I had in my first book, *Layoffs and Hope*, regarding big companies that are like dinosaurs. Either they learn to act like small companies and efficiently produce value-added products and services and be in compliance with the re-invented American Global Capitalism, or they are on their way to extinction.

Writing this part of the book reminded me of the heated discussion I had with the Byrd at the basement of that student radio station in Stanford University. "Bruce, put your American pride aside and admit that Capitalism is dead! It is as dead as a doorknob! Accept it and do not fight it!" He said these words only to be target of my most fierce rejection attack of his ideas.

However, some three years later and publishing three books, it seems like I have made peace with what he was saying. The old Capitalism is dead all right but it is replaced by the reinvented 21st century American Global Capitalism. AGC will make the world respect and like America as a leader. When the global population sees America doing what America is supposed to do then they will all be on our side; when they see that America is helping them feed their kids and put food on their tables; when they see the new proactive profitable philanthropy they will be converts to our freedom and democracy. This will be an all compassing freedom and democracy that is by far cheaper in dollars and human life and blood payments; this will be some everlasting honest freedom and democracy subject to their culture and customs that no barrel of gun could ever instill or enforce!

Imagine if we stopped the idea of "taking by force" the wealth of the top 1% and distributed it among 99%, Imagine if we like Brazil told our CEOs and the 99% greed is American and is human as long as they follow the AGC rules. Imagine if that 99% was individually just as wealthy as each of the 1%! Trust me, the unlimited American material and capital augmented by limitless intellectual resources can and will do this. Instead of being cheap and requiring maddening government enforced austerity and that miserable misery index of the old and dead Capitalism, we instill prosperity. There is more than enough for everyone!

Please Contact: bruce@razban.com

CHAPTER 8
Future: Digital Humanity, Digital Economy, and Human Intellectual Property

In my senior year at the University of Wisconsin, in 1970, I was privileged to take the Electrical Engineering course, EE454. Professor Donald Dietmeyer, who had a great deal of experience working at IBM, was our most respected professor. He knew what he was talking about, and was a superb teacher. His students were mesmerized by how well he could describe things that were complicated for them to understand. Being his Ph.D. student was the most coveted opportunity for any graduate student.

He started the course by telling us that everything in a digital world can be one of, and only one of, two things. It can be either true, or it can be false. There is nothing in the middle, and there are no exceptions.

Professor Dietmeyer agreed to be my Ph.D. advisor, and this made other graduate students envious. Unfortunately, I did not complete the Ph. D., although I had done all the class work and even had a Ph. D. thesis topic selected.

Let's fast forward some forty or fifty years.

A re-invented global capitalism has taken us by devastating surprise. This re-invented capitalism manifested itself in huge drops in the Wall Street stocks in 2008. It has also been showing itself in most misunderstood situations, without any success.

Just like Professor Dietmeyer's anything can be true or false, the entire world now is forced to make a choice. This choice is obvious and easy to understand, yet consequences of denying it can be horrendous. Just like that, anything can be true or false. America is now asked, "Are you a first class, first-world leader, or are you a third-world country?" The urgency and all-consuming impact of it makes us feel like being in crosshairs, as well as being at a serious crossroads. One wrong move and we might be finished as the world leader and become a third world country. This is similar to the way Israelis have felt being surrounded by enemies all these years. They had to win, otherwise they would be finished.

In *Layoffs and Hope*, there is a chapter that says the world expects America to be America and lead. Now, some three years after that, I think that this has become even more threatening.

Dr. Kubler-Ross's book on death and dying, which she

based on decades of research, talks about the different stages one goes through before accepting death. Anger, denial, negotiations, and finally acceptance are some of the steps that I remember.

The anger stage was Democrats being angry at Republicans and Republicans being mutually angry at Democrats. Another manifestation was the self-damnation that we, as Americans, spent too much, borrowed too much, and were so stupid that our companies have to mass import not only cheap labor, but also IT engineers from India.

We internalized this the same way that a laid off employee does. We thought that there must definitely be something wrong with us for letting this happen. We were at fault! This ignited a shame and blame game unprecedented in American history. I know this psychological effect well. I have sadly seen it at work with laid-off employees.

During an interview for this book, a colleague who had been unemployed for almost three years told me, "Mr. Razban, look around you in Silicon Valley. About eighty to ninety percent of employees are recent arrivals from India and China. In some companies, everyone is a recent arrival. Look around you. There is an anti-American discrimination in our own country! Did you ever go to a car rental place in El Camino in Sunnyvale on a Monday morning? I tell you, most are fresh-arrival Indians and Chinese with a perfect FICA score of 810, while Americans cannot buy cars."

My argument that these are future generation Americans, and America is nation of immigrants, did not go too far.

He interrupted me by saying, "Bruce I had to declare bankruptcy 12 hours before the bank was going to auction my house. How do you expect me to accept job loss when they are hiring by the truckload from India and China? Did you know that Apple has hired 100,000 employees in China? Did you know that a lot of American companies are putting their headquarters in Zug, in Switzerland, to avoid paying taxes? Do you know that all these things kill jobs?"

My research for *Layoffs and Hope* proved to me that America needs jobs, jobs, jobs, jobs! I was elated to see that Vice President Biden said exactly the same thing about a year and a half after the book was published. Serving the White House as a Silicon Valley community leader, it again became clear to us that the answer was jobs, jobs, jobs, jobs!

A scientific Six Sigma analysis clearly indicates that the root cause of all these difficulties is that the average citizen is having a hard time putting food on the table or keeping a roof over the heads of his/her family. This finding is global. It was the same thing that started the Arab Spring, even though it turned into a bloody civil war in Libya and Syria. Of course, citizens' demands for freedom are just as fundamental as food. Yet, the same problems that almost started a civil war in Arab countries, yet thanks God peaceful, revolt in Israel over the price of cottage cheese.

It's now a given that the digital "true or false" that Prof. Dietmeyer taught has become the dominant universal "truth." In fact, it goes beyond this. Imagine a politician being elected or deposed instantly based on real-time statistics. Imagine that an election promise that was left unfulfilled can now become instant mass knowledge with our social media. Imagine that each employee's salary can vary from hour to hour depending on his/her real value-added work towards generating human intellectual and material capital wealth. Imagine that CEOs were kept digitally accountable for their performance in the office. Imagine that based on some statistical simulation, we were able to accurately predict an economic "bubble" from creation to its death, and prevent massive job losses and global displacement and economic instability. Imagine that big companies, instead of going away like dinosaurs, become more community-conscious and keep job creation and destruction as one of their operating matrices. Imagine that instead of the hundred or more year old Adam Smith misery index for the old material-based economy, we now use material and human intellectual property as an index or metric. Imagine that instead of the wide-spread resentment towards CEOs and corporations, CEOs take the lead and create American jobs for Americans. Warren Buffett is an American hero for doing exactly this. Imagine that America, given the choice between being a third-world country or an ultra-power, becomes a globally re-invested capitalist nation that is respected by the entire world.

This is a role that America is destined to have. China cannot, because they do not have the democratic infrastructure and there is limited freedom, even though they have become a respected nation, world-wide, for making progress in all these areas. Economic dislocation and instability will devour many of their impressive accomplishments. America is lucky to have such stiff competition from India, China, and Brazil! This will help

America rise from ashes.

America, like Japan, which was hit with some of the most awful natural disasters recently, will succeed. America, like Israel, which has had to live with one of the most unstable regions in the world, will succeed.

In August of 2013, BBC had a news item indicating the Chinese students and graduates were going to Buddhist temples to pray for jobs. This is what we teach in our graduate courses as an unwritten contract. The unwritten contract is something that has been working for some years and it holds responsible several parties that certain commitment and accomplishment from one party will deliver rewards from another group. For example, if a student studies hard and gets a good education than the society and community is responsible in return to give that student a good job that makes all the good things in life possible.

This report in addition to depicting the difficulties of Chinese as well other nationals in getting good jobs, it says also something very important. It says tht the Chinese government, as any other responsible government is worried that there will not be enough of good and meaningful jobs for their graduates.

As you might recall, China's economy was expanding at a rate of near 10% for some time. Unfortunately, it slowed down around 2010 or so.

This is not a Chinese only problem. This is a world-wide problem that our leaders and government will soon realize that they have to work on. Jobs are the foundation of our economy. We must on a global basis plan and make sure that jobs are there for anyone who is willing and able to work. Without these jobs out economy will falter and as we have seen in the aftermath of the Global Financial Crisis, then this inability to produce meaningful jobs will undoubtedly result in the breaking of the fabric of our societies as we know them.

Internet and what will be presented later as Click University, will be instrumental to make sure students are getting marketable, certifiable skill set in time for the market.

This is why universities such as DeVry and Keller Graduate School of management, Phoenix, and UC San Francisco will excel since they are career universities that have professors who have had that crucial industry careers and who are teaching experience and not just some theory.

To maintain our primary or standby careers we must

constantly update and upgrade our skill set.

On the next subject, I must say that I am a bit biased. That subject is Brazil. I think that they are resource-rich, like us. Yet, I think that their soccer (football) team is far better than ours or any other country in the world. In addition, Brazil has done better than us by letting their management win. In return, their management has been accountable and transparent. Government and business are allies...

Perhaps we need to learn from India on how to harness our human intellectual capital. Maybe we can learn from their lack of respect and envy when it comes to materialism obsessed fixation.

We, on the other hand, are hit with too many financial and business problems right now. This brings up a bitter lesson I have learned all these years as an unofficial coach, helping those who are unemployed in the last thirty years. Unemployment eventually creates domestic, family, psychological, and physical health problems. I have seen suicides that happened because a productive person was cut off from their work and feeling of productivity. I have seen divorces happen to couples who would have otherwise not gotten the divorce if it was not for unemployment, foreclosures, and/or layoffs.

So, what has been the side-effect of this massive digital revolution? Well, there are some great things like Facebook, Twitter, or Google. However, wrongly used, these all can backfire and create an awful situation for the globe.

Please Contact: bruce@razban.com

CHAPTER 9
Should We Drink This Indian J2EE Java?

During my graduate years at the University of Wisconsin in Madison, I met Mr. Ramachandra Reddy. Those days, Mr. Reddy was a household name for a detergent. One day, I saw writing on the common board for graduate students that read, "Hello, I am Mr. Reddy, and I will share desk number four with you!" Mr. Reddy, who liked to joke about being the famous Mr. Reddy, had arrived.

He was a graduate of the Indian Institute of Technology, or IIT, which is their equivalent of MIT. This is a topnotch institute that only admits the best of the best and the brightest of the brightest, and puts them through the best technology training available anywhere in the world.

What soon became clear to all of us was that Mr. Reddy was miles ahead of all of us. Not only he was super-intelligent, but he studied extremely hard and he had had an excellent background at IIT. What is remarkable is that he was also highly humble and genuinely caring. We soon became fast friends and took similar classes together in preparation of the Ph.D., since we both had the honor of becoming Professor Dietmeyer's coveted graduate students. Professor Dietmeyer, as you might recall, is the IBM professional who taught us the first digital course. We started working for him right after he returned from a logic design conference in Israel.

Unfortunately, neither of us did complete the degree. In my case, I revolted against the Electrical Engineering Department and gave the entire graduate body a lecture on how the Ph.D. program needed to be updated at Wisconsin to compete with MIT and Stanford. I had learned a great deal from the antiwar talks and lectures in the campus. I am highly proud of my Wisconsin world-class education from two points of view. One was that I got a great education in the classrooms. The second was that by being around students from all parts of the globe, I learned to have an open mind and be a practitioner of international good will and understanding. I paid a price for this. The price was that engineering discipline is extremely concentrated and focused on technical things. The stereotypical engineering student was something similar to the nerds that you see in TV shows. At that time I was the renegade and outcast, since I loved taking psychology and other classes,

55

especially management, and, more important, I was involved in social activities. Chinese and Indian students in general were smarter and better educated in their undergraduate studies. They made competition really difficult.

Just like Mr. Reddy, I had a Chinese friend, Mr. Larry T. Chang. He had adopted me when he felt really sorry for me. He felt sorry for me since I was working extremely hard. But, with his caring wisdom and kind voice, he told me that I was studying too many things. "You are studying things that are not important at the expense of those which are." This was his advice, and both Mr. Reddy and I knew that we needed to listen to this upper classman who had our best interests at heart.

One day in 1995, I was asked by my boss, Conrad DeLetis, Vice President of IT at National Semiconductor Corporation, to meet a Sun Microsystems delegation who wanted to talk about "Hot Java!" There had been some movies where the movie stars referred to coffee as Java in saying let us go get a hot cup of Java!" However, since I was keeping up with all the latest technology, I was relatively familiar with Java as the latest programming language, invented by James Gusseling right there on the Stanford Campus, which I visited often. The important thing is that at first James named this new language Acorn since there was a tree right outside his office at Stanford, and squirrels were usually running around and feasting on fresh acorns. I met James in some Java One conferences, along with Bill Joy. These two are among the highest dignitaries of high-tech. I had also read about Object-Oriented programming, and read two books, written by one Israeli and one American author.

In that Hot Java meeting, I was instrumental in convincing the VP that Java was good stuff and it would help us from a technical point of view. Java soon took off like wildfire.

At that time, most technical people thought that Java was invented in India. This is false. Ever since in 1958, when IBM introduced the concept of SUBROUTINE in the FORTRAN programming language, a Java-like concept was invented to encapsulate different parts of the program from each other. In 1971, in one of the programming classes at the University of Wisconsin, we were introduced to the concept of structured programming, which is another basis for Java.

However, from that fateful 1995 meeting in Conrad DeLetis's office regarding Hot Java, until many years later, Sun

Microsystems kept spending millions and millions of dollars on Java.

Many colleges, and even some high schools, were teaching Java to their students, and it was possible to get a Java certificate.
Unfortunately, as Americans, we were not that good in getting international patents to protect our technology. We worked extremely hard and gave away the technology for free.

Still, to this day, many of the new innovations come from America.

India was smart. They decided to take a chance and dive headfirst into Java. Soon there was an invasion of Indian new arrivals in Silicon Valley as Java gurus. Some companies would be 48% new arrivals from India, and another 48% new arrivals from China leaving the remaining 4% for rest of the world. In addition, a good 85% of recruiters in high-tech were either Indians or Chinese.

Soon there were departments in companies that were almost completely Indian or Chinese. Americans were quickly becoming a minority in their own country, and at the receiving end of discrimination. While California was and is suffering from 12% unemployment, there seem to be daily arrivals of Indians and Chinese using the H1 Visa. Google, for instance, hired a new employee from Hungary and paid his entire travel expenses so he could take the new employee orientation class. This was happening right where there was a 50% unemployment rate among Americans who were 50 or older, and a full 27% unemployment among Americans in the 18 to 25 age bracket. This alarmingly high unemployment was for the white. Sadly, other Americans, especially minorities, were experiencing double the above figures.

CEOs were "importing cheap labor," in their minds. They were thinking, "Why should I pay an American market rate when I can hire two fresh arrivals from India or China for the same price?" Unfortunately, this is a false assumption. This is because massive importation of cheap labor created double-digit American unemployment. Our calculations show that even the so-called American 4% unemployment costs American industry, government, community, and humanity a cool $2.4 trillion a year. So, while the CEO calculations to stockholders and Wall Street were trumpeting a saving, it drained the entire monetary echo system, causing irreparable damage to everybody and everything.

Let me tell you that I am not a Democrat or Republican

anymore. However, I can be branded as a Reagan Republican, or a Clinton Democrat. I am now a proud American, because I was honored to be asked to be a Silicon Valley community leader working on job creation for the White House. I am of the firm opinion that when your country calls for you to serve, you do the best that you can to serve.

I am of the opinion that President Obama is one huge reason for America to be respected in the world as the leader again. Also, I hope and pray that President Obama will be another John F. Kennedy.

This parallelism is strengthened in my mind because of the Cuba Crisis and dumping of cheap steel that happened during the John F. Kennedy administration. We, as Americans, stood up then, and we can stand up again. Also remember that we were the first to send a man to the moon.

You might be thinking that I am not in favor of bringing foreigners, which are future Americans to this country. This is not true, since I, too, was a foreigner. However, in order to get a job, and later become a citizen, I had to follow the American law that made sure no American would lose their job if I got the job.

The importation of Indian and Chinese nationals to replace Americans in the workplace is so massive that even some of the older Indians who are US Citizens are alarmed.

"Bruce, this is not good for Indians. These fresh new Indians come here and get huge salaries, while the gap between the haves and have-nots is getting so wide that some poverty-stricken Indian farmers are committing suicide." This was what an old Indian friend told me.

Am I angry at Indians? No! However, we as Americans need to better manage our lives and work so as not have this type of job invasion that resulted in 12% unemployment in Silicon Valley! We must hold our heads up and plan and execute our plans to beat the Indian invasion by American know-how! What should we do if we come across gross discrimination in the work place?

Answer: send email to ceo@companyname.com (where you have to substitute the actual company name). Send letters to the CEOs and complain. There was a big billboard in Madison, Wisconsin during the height of the Vietnam War that said, "Your Silence is Killing Us!" Go to www.google.com, find the name of company CEO, and call or send them a certified letter. Protest peacefully, and speak up! We, as American consumers, do have a great deal of power.

The other thing is that as a US patent holder, I am angrily aware of violations of American patents by other countries, and even inside our country.

However, the India of Taj Mahal; the India of Mohandas, Dr. Gandhi the leader of peaceful protest; the India of one of the most ancient democracies has a special place in my thinking. India has single handedly proven my point that intellectual Capitalism is just as important as materials Capitalism.

I strongly recommend that we extended the most sincere welcome to the new arrivals from India and give them the best legal protection that American law can provide hoping they will be the next generation of patriotic Americans. These people are workers just like you and me who are trying to get work. The fundamental problem is the imbalance that such massive import/export has created on a global basis. The real issue is that these new arrivals are just as victims as Americans are in their own country.

Forgive me for saying this: All of us, in a collective and global sense have done what is a Forrest Gump saying that "Stupid is What Stupid Does!" Had we better managed this, we could have somehow maintained the delicate global balance to optimize collective gains and minimized collective losses.

Let us think of positive things. Peter Seeger is a famous folk's singer. I would play again and again his song Guantanamera.

In an interview that is documented in youtube.com he points out that he is optimistic about the future partially because of Internet. "Before Internet, you would have one man trying to solve problems in the US and he would do his best and tries very hard to solve that problem all by himself. Now, with Internet and the women revolution, a woman in America who is trying to solve a problem will find others in India and the entire globe and says let us solve this together for the benefit of the entire world."

As you have seen in this book, we are in digital age. This is point that Pete Seeger tries to make emphatically. He says, agriculture age took thousands of years to become mature, industrial age took hundreds of years. But the digital age has taken only decades and the impact has been much more powerful."

But, according to him, we have to stabilize things. We live in a global world where everyone is interdependent on the others and communication via Internet happens at the speed of light. This will then help us to move at the speed of light towards implementing digital humanity; managing not only material capital but also human and intellectual capital.

As mentioned before, our entire materials-only based system is based on the fact that we think greed is good. Then it adds that human needs are ever increasing. But then the materials-based economy quickly adds that materials on earth are in short supply. Therefore, our economic system is based on scarcity. This means that there are only limited materials and once we use them, those materials are gone. Now, let us contrast this to the world human intellectual capability where inventiveness and ideas are absolutely limitless. In fact the more we use our intellectual capability, the more there is to use for the "Philanthropic Profitability!" Let me humbly say that this last expression of philanthropic profitability is my invention!

I want to make this perfectly clear that America is a land of diversity; America is land of immigrants; America welcomes new immigrants. However, with the massive importation of newly arrivals "cheap labor" to replace American jobs, we find this unacceptable because this crashes stability both in the US by increasing unemployment among Americans, and creates a brain drain in other countries where the best and most talented abandon their homeland to come to the US.

In fact, I strongly believe that these new immigrants are just as victims as the unemployed Americans are. All of this is due to bad management. Furthermore, good management is what can fix this serious global economic condition!

Please Contact: bruce@razban.com

CHAPTER 10
Is China our Friend or Foe?

Donald Trump was saying in 2011 that China was eating our lunch. At the same time, in a CNN interview with Piers Morgan, The CEO of Starbucks was saying, "China is a customer, and we have opened many branches in mainland China and other places."

Others tend to think that China is out to destroy America as a superpower and replace it. Others think that China is a friend.

My reading is that:

- China is the biggest manufacturing superpower. We are not able or want to dislodge them in manufacturing.
- China is an electronics manufacturing giant, with huge human resources.
- For now, China is not able to do completely creative and innovative things like we do effortlessly in Silicon Valley.
- China has come a long way from Tiananmen Square incident.
- China is trying to become a respected world community member and put Tiananmen Square behind them.

Thus, I arrive at the conclusion that we need to respect China and India. Beyond that, we must find ways of working with them in a fair win-win and constructive fashion.

Respecting and working with China is as American as apple pie. This is true even though the pie pan might say "Made in China." Remember that the apple used for this pie might be from one of those seeds that Johnny Appleseed planted.

It is critically important to make sure that we, as Americans, have to have our guard up. Sadly, we owe a great deal to China. On the other side, China needs to treat America well, since America is its best customer. There is a strong need for both sides to respect and cooperate with each other. We must arrive at a win-win situation via mutual trust loyalty and fair and honest teamwork. Perhaps we can learn from China and imitate their imitation of our reinvented AGC before it is too late!

Call me a dreamer, China is not only not our enemy, China is that great dose of reality check and China is that potential most powerful business and economy partner.

I do know that a lot my respected readers at this point

would like to challenge me on the point I just made and fairly so. I painfully know that there are executives and American leaders who are saying "China is eating our lunch!"

What if we communicated and worked and cooperated with them? What if instead of saying that China by keeping their currency artificially low causes 1,000,000 American jobs, we offered them some incentive so they somehow helped us regain that 1,000,000 jobs, while they got something equivalent as well?

While the fact is that China is an economic, industrial, and even military superpower, we need to treat China almost the same way treated Japan.

In general we know that competition is good in an open market. Also, from a management point of view we know that there are advantages to have smart competition such as China, India, Japan, and Brazil as well as others. This smart competition helps us to be on our toes and use our American know how and ingenuity, hopefully in alliance with our competition to produce outstanding results.

China has come a long way from before even though their super fast growth cannot and will not continue at the same rate. Yet they are open to many Western ideas that they were not some few years ago. This opening in China and elsewhere is a golden opportunity for us to become their partners and create a win-win economy and strong interdependence.

In my teaching graduating MBA students, I am honored to have international students from many countries and cultures including China. I find a genuine interest in these students to really understand not just American technology and education, but American way of life. As we study organization cultures in these classes, my Chinese and Indian students quickly realize what is good for Americans in America and what works here may or may not work exactly the same way back in their home country.

In a way a lot of my international students have the opportunity to get best of both worlds. They are lucky enough to pick and choose the best things in each culture and country as it applies to their own case to adapt a new way of superior life that cannot be achieved by only one country or one culture.

In addition, I greatly admire the ancient cultures of China, Japan, and India. They have been around a lot longer than us and they have learned, in their way a lot more than us.

Let me give you an example. In business trip to Japan, I

discovered that one of our most important customers had developed a test product that seemed highly similar to our product. Upon my return and before the jetlag was gone, I was ordered to meet with a high-level committee. Drinking several double espressos one after the other, I had finally gotten rid of my sleepiness and related jetlag problems.

Meeting started with, "Mr. Razban, thanks for this business trip. We like to hear your thoughts. Please be as frank as you can since this is an important case for our company!" During the course of discussion and testimonials of technical, management, and marketing professionals it became obvious that there was a strong resemblance between our product and the one that had the logo of the other company on it. I first thoughts were that there will be a legal action.

There was no legal action and we were all asked to keep absolutely quiet about this.

Much to my surprise, the offending product was being sold in Japan and there was no legal objection from my company.

Then, suddenly there was a major announcement. Another Japanese company had decided to adopt one of our products with a trade valuation very close to total sell of the disputed product. The mutual trust and loyalty between our executives and the other Japanese company and the fact that there had been a strong business relationship for a number of years had created a win-win situation. This win-win was not only an American style, but it was based on a strong leadership and management that understood world management practices and put them to great use.

Please Contact: bruce@razban.com

CHAPTER 11
Viva Brazil, Shalom Israel, Viva France, UK, and Konichava Japan!

More than China and India, among the most progressive nations, my most favorite is Brazil. Brazil is in the Americas, and therefore somewhat more familiar and similar to us in culture and business. Like us, they have immense resources. However, unlike us, they have been expanding their economy. It's also important to note that their economic expansion has not been at our expense.

I must make a confession at this point. I love their soccer (football) team. Some years ago, when they beat the American team really badly in Stanford Stadium, I was cheering them along with their fanatic fans with half their faces painted blue and the other half yellow, beating their bongos in synchronous rhythm. I loved the contingent of bongo and drum players that go with them, at their own expense, for many games.

Keeping this in mind, Brazil seems to have made a practical and productive win-win alliance arrangement between government and business to successfully fuel their expansion engine.

"I do not care how much the CEOs make. So long as they keep people working, we do the best we can to help them!" This is what the Brazilian president said in an interview.

Israel has been the only Middle East democracy, and it has been our staunch and dependable friend. Most impressively, they have had to learn how to work with constant and permanent crisis, and even outright hatred. This is one thing that we can learn, and work with them to improve our ability to live, or even thrive, in these turbulent times. Their high-tech industry is very similar to ours. We need to find out what makes them successful in spite all these wars and setbacks. We need to learn how to live in a dangerous world, like they had to.

There is one obvious lesson that we can learn from Israelis. When Gilatt Shalit, an Israeli soldier was captured and kept hostage for five years, Israel did not give up. In the Israeli Army, there is saying that "We do not leave our soldiers behind!" A friend who is a project manager and consultant told me, "Bruce at this point our management is such that we send our employees to the present economic battle field to defend us. This is just like a commander sending her soldiers in front of live bullets. And, then when they get hit, instead of going to their rescue, we ask them why they are bleeding!" Finally, I got what was trying to tell me. He was saying that in business just like in battle field we must protect and defend our employees (soldiers). Maybe soon American business titans learn that they have to have the mutual trust and loyalty of their employees, by giving them mutual trust and loyalty.

France has made huge strides under Sarkozy. There are indications that France wants to be a real American friend and ally. It stands to reason for us to become their partner and help them become a superpower while we are making progress in becoming the global ultra power.

UK, America's motherland, is unique and very dear to us. By linking our economies even more than before, we could have a win-win situation that is unparalleled in the world. I'll never forget when our national anthem was played, by Her Majesty the Queen's order, in her palace as a measure of solidarity with us after the 9/11 terrorist attacks.

I have travelled to Japan many times on business, and I am in love with the Japanese culture and business. Konichava means hello, or good day.

When the devastating Tsunami hit Japan, it really broke my heart. However, as in the past, I'm positive that this time, too, Japan and the Japanese will survive and thrive again. It might take a few years. Since we are both hit really bad, we can become very close allies. I am referring to their Tsunami and Earthquake disaster and our economic and business disaster. Of course, theirs was a Mother Nature massive disruption and ours economic or mismanagement.

Japan is a land of ancient culture and extremely high value system. Up to recently, when a CEO of a Japanese company messed up and caused massive job loss, he would get in front of the entire company and resign. This is in fact in sharp contrast to some company CEOs messing up a company; resigning and using their golden parachute and go to another company; get a raise and mess them up too again and again get another promotion and go to yet another company!

You might be questioning the benefit of this chapter. The real benefit of this chapter is that the world has become a tiny global village, and we need to do a lot of teamwork to succeed. Every decision, every action, every upheaval, every event in any part of the globe, now affects everybody else in the entire digital humanity, at Internet speed.

In addition, our technology enables and empowers us to do the right things and be rewarded for it, or do the wrong things and be devastatingly punished for it. For example,

- Working our workers as hard as possible and not fairly rewarding them, might quickly result in a Facebook and Twitter revolt organized against the offending companies, boards of directors, and CEOs!

- Using the Google, "Do no harm" model, in general, what is suggested in this book as a way of making a lot of money which is "Proactive Profitable Philanthropy," and we will have a financial reward that is awesome.

- Manage our companies well and in an honest and transparent way and people will wait in line to buy our products and services.

- Do massive and frequent layoffs and no one will want to work for us, even those bootlegged cheap laborers from other countries. They are smart enough to know that soon they will also lose their jobs in a foreign country, and be left with nothing.

- Cultivate and develop outstanding mutual trust and loyalty among our workers, management, and customers; develop superior products, and we'll soon see the magic of viral marketing work for us. In this case, our products will sell themselves!

Please Contact: bruce@razban.com

CHAPTER 12
The Entire Globe Must Declare War on Global Unemployment!

I have no doubt that if we go into another recession, one alternative is for the government to declare a state of emergency and declare war on job loss in a global sense. I'm sad to report that America is fighting three wars now; Iraq, Afghanistan, and the financial crisis.

While social networks, developed in Silicon Valley facilitated the Arab Spring, nothing less than a declaration of war on joblessness, on a global scale, can help us recover.

The Global Financial Crisis is a serious business crisis. Massive and frequent layoffs and poor management, along with a silent re-invention of Capitalism, makes it necessary for all of us to join hands in dealing with such a travesty, challenge, and opportunity.

In management and business, we do the six sigma analysis. With this analysis, we do our best to separate major causes of a problem from the secondary effects. We try to quickly determine the major sources of problems rather than trying to hide or diminish the causes. I'm sure you've heard the expression, "Moving furniture on *Titanic's* deck" in an effort to prevent the primary problem, namely the sinking of the ship, with superficial efforts such as moving the furniture.

It's important to note that unemployment was and continues to be, the primary source of all the financial difficulties; it's the main reason for the Arab Spring; it's the main reason for the uprising in UK. People need to know that they can put bread on the table; people need to know that their work is respected; people need to know that future is bright.

The second most important thing is that money is only useful when it is circulating! Right now, many of the super-rich Americans, as well as some corporations, are sitting on huge amounts of money, and are too scared to spend it in creating jobs. This is the same fear that is devastating the workers in their lack of job security; the same fear that allows an employer to terminate an employee "at will," and allows an employee to pick up and leave at will. This fear is responsible for a major demise of trust and loyalty.

The third most important thing is that human capital

needs to be respected with just as much care as material capital.

Just to put this in perspective, let quote what was said in Devos Annual Meeting in Switzerland in 2004. This is an important international meeting where many CEOs attend to exchange ideas and in fact set the directions for the future. In that meeting the moderator, Larry Summers was trying to predict how the business world would be in 2014.

Larry pointed out that there are five categories of resources that each company, regardless of being big or small has. In his outlook, he pointed at these categories as physical, (which is referred to as materials capital in my book), human capital, Intellectual Property (IP), culture, and the network of relationships with the community and other companies. I am very glad to see that there is a good agreement between what he says and what has been my conclusion.

Going back to my list, the fourth is that the Internet is providing and demanding that things happen at the speed of light. The Internet requires that information that is available everywhere and instantly must be integrated and considered in all the government, business, and individual activities in real time, and be completely transparent.

Going back to that Devos conference, Carly Fiorina added that the importance on materials capital is becoming less and less important as importance of the all four other categories increases. She points out that there are three pillars on which a company, organization, or even individual rest. These are competitiveness, competition, and character. She also expands on my idea of importance of Internet and points out that all processes and procedures are becoming digital, mobile, and virtual. All the above considerations bring us to the new reality that is Digital Humanity.

Digital Humanity means that we, as human beings, will now have to do effective teamwork with the digital age.

Penalties for not doing this will be disastrous. Rewards for doing this can be monumental!

Please Contact: bruce@razban.com

CHAPTER 13
How to Inspire and Empower Ourselves to Thrive in Turbulent Economic Times

In one of the *Peanuts* cartoon strips, Snoopy recalls that he had to work hard in school. Then he says that he studied hard so he can get a degree. Once he had a degree, he could get a good job. Once he had a good job, he worked hard to succeed. He formed a family and had children. He sent his kids to school to studied hard and get a degree so they get a good job. Then they could have children of their own who could work hard, too. I have often asked myself, "Working hard, but working hard for what?" I love Snoopy cartoons.

This one struck me hard. I had seen this when I was in college. Unfortunately, it did not quite sink in until I had about twenty years of work experience. Then, I realized that I had just worked, paid the bills, and bought things. I worked, and worked hard, and saw time – and indeed life itself – walk on by. Being part of the sandwich generation, I had to pay for my parents and my kid. I worked, I made lots of money, I paid bills, but my life was empty. I was not doing my passion and mission, and therefore I lived an unhappy work life.

One day, I had a heart attack at work. This happened at the peak of my career and I did not even realize that this was a heart attack.

I didn't bother to take half a day off and check into some Emergency Room. I was too busy making sure that I did not get fired. There was so much back-stabbing that I did not dare take any time off. It was not until six months later, in a routine physical checkup, the Doctor came up with the criminal accusation that I must have had a heart attack.

In a condescending way, the doctor almost yelled at me, "Bruce, it is absolutely clear. Look at your EKG! You had a heart attack." Then he went on lecturing on his soap box and asked me why I did not go to the Emergency Room right away. "Mr. Razban, your father was a doctor. What were you thinking?" This added salt to the wound that I did not need.

The truth is that I did not care! I had become one of those zombies in a toxic work place.

At the age fifty-three, I was working hard for the day that I could afford the best for my loved ones. I was thinking, *someday!*

I was thinking that someday everything will be OK. I had to survive that God-awful job for that day, that week, that month, my entire career, and then live happily ever after.

I had a vacation and cruise brochure tucked inside the glove compartment of my Lexus. I even had a plan to be on vacation about a month after my heart attack. Unfortunately, the heart attack ruined the day, the month, the year, and the preplanned vacation. I lost a considerable amount of money to the airline, since I did not cancel my ticket.

Each day, I had dutifully gone to work. Each day, I had tried to navigate my way without rocking the boat. Each day, I had followed orders, just like a zombie. Each day of this hard working had caused a little of me and my soul to die. So much of me had died that I did not care. I just needed the paycheck to take care of my family and pay the bills.

The horrendous commute each day would make me more and more depressed and angry. The toxic work environment had taken all my energy and drained me of my enthusiasm, jovial self, and inventiveness.

Come to think of it, my dad, the doctor, worked hard, too. He worked extremely hard. I remember that when I was a child, he would be called in the middle of night and go to the hospital to take care of a patient.

He worked very hard, but he was happy! He did not complain. He would buy the latest textbooks in his field just to stay competent. I started to think about this. My dad and I both worked hard, but his hard and difficult work invigorated him while my hard work was killing me. The difference was that his job was his life-long passion, and mine was the opposite.

On one of those rainy commute hour fiascos, I started to really see what made him click. My grandfather was killed in some forgotten war when my dad was only four years old. My dad had to fight with poverty all his life. My grandmother, a very strong, smart woman, had to work hard too. She was cleaning houses, mending and tailoring clothes, and taught in the evenings and weekends, just to make ends meet and put my dad through medical school. Her hard work was a labor of love, so her son would become that proverbial Jewish doctor. His hard work was so he got the degree as a doctor and treated those who could not afford it. He was determined not to let patients who were poor go without medication or treatment, like he had to when he was a child. He was the chief doctor in a hospital in Tehran that took care of the poorest of the poor.

One night he came home late. My mother told him that she could not put up with tightly budgeted spending regimen that they had to keep, since my dad's income from the hospital was just not enough to pay all the bills. He resigned from the poverty-stricken hospital and went to a hospital that catered to the wealthy. His income increased by fifty or more percent. Unfortunately, his spirits had dampened by hundred and fifty percent.

Soon, we bought a new car and got to do the ignored repair to the house. My mother bought some nice clothes for my dad. Unfortunately, he was not himself any more. He went to work a bit late and he returned a bit early. He did not seem to be in his jovial mood any more.

One day, my mother told us that she had an announcement to make before we could start our dinner. She started by saying to my father, "I know that you used to be a lot happier before, when you worked for the hospital for the indigent. I also know that you do not quite enjoy working in the new hospital. Is this true?"

My dad tried to hedge the answer. "Not really," was the faint answer he gave my mother, so as not to get involved in an argument with her. With a triumphant smile and a sort of choked up voice, she added that "Well, Doctor Razban, I have good news for you! Your resignation letter was not accepted by the charity group that ran the hospital. You have to go back to the hospital for the poor where you loved so much to work!"

My dad, trying to get all of this in, asked my mother to repeat what she had just said. Then, playing with the food on his brand new plate that the money from the wealthy hospital had provided, he said this is the best thing that could have happened to him. "A man who says no to money finds a freedom that no amount of money can ever buy!" was my dad's lesson to his children.

Next day, and the days after that, we saw that my dad was getting happier each day that he went to his charity hospital. My dad was a much happier man. He had found his mission and passion in life, regardless of money. As these memories were keeping my mind occupied, I remembered the book called *What Color is Your Parachute?* This master piece book was written by Richard Bolles, affectionately known as Mr. B.

What Color is Your Parachute is the bible for job seekers. In my consulting practice, I had used his ideas extensively when I was in between consulting gigs and without a paycheck.

Finally, this book shed light on what made my dad have a happy work life. He had a mission and a passion. In fact he was lucky that his mission and passion; his work and play were one and the same! His mission was to be a doctor who treated the poorest of the poor and tell them that they only had to pay whatever they could, if anything. His mission was to beg for free medication samples from his colleagues and drug manufaturers and cheerfully dispense them to the poor. This way, they did not have to suffer what my dad had to when he was sick and they could not afford the treatment. This mission had created a passion for him. The passion was to become the best of the best doctors that there could be. His papers, published in medical journals, earned him a trip to Paris to lecture in Centre International des Enfant to tell the world, and tell them proudly as the Iranian representative working in a charity hospital about his latest discovery. When there was a standing ovation at the end, he had made part of his mission accomplished.

"Mr. Bruce Razban, what really is your mission? What do you think about your work-life related passion?" This was what I honestly asked myself, as if I had the answer. The honest answer was that I really did not have any. You, too, might pause and think about what your job, career, and/or life mission and passions are. My heart attack was a good teacher. My work from then on had to have a mission and passion. My wife, who is an Israeli who had to serve in two wars, had already figured out my mission. "Bruce, you want to help people have a better work life. You're a coach. You are a teacher. I see the intense happiness in your eyes when you help someone recover from being fired or laid off." Then she added, "You even went to a colleague's house to help him put together a resume and start searching for a job. You were happy as hell that day. You were much happier than when you found that you were given a big raise in the job that eventually gave you a heart attack."

She had made her case, and she had to rush to bring our daughter home from school.

Was this really true? Yes it was. I was flying on cloud nine when this guy finally got a job. It had taken a long time to mentally prepare him to update his resume and start the work search ordeal. Nevertheless, he had done it.

I could not take credit. Somehow, through the grace of God, I was able to tell him the right words to sooth his anger and depression for being unfairly terminated. These words helped him realize that he was not "damaged goods," and he could be fine again in the workplace. Then, once I knew that I had his attention, I told him "Well, I, too, was fired, and fired unfairly!" He jumped out of his chair and almost out of his skin with relief that he was not the only one who had been fired unfairly. Then as if wanting to cherish the moment, he asked me to repeat this for his wife to hear. I did that. I had tried to help others almost at the expense of losing my own job, at times.

That did not mean anything. My mission was to help others with their work life! Like a soldier, my war was to help those who had lost their jobs get back on their feet and go back to work.

When a cashier who had purchased one of the first copies of the *Layoffs & Hope* told me that this book has saved her son's life, I took that as a figure of speech. I was just as happy as my dad was during the standing ovation at that medical seminar. However, that lady, my fan number one, had more to say. "Mr. Razban, you really saved him. I did not mean his job, you saved him. My son is back. He is alive again. Thank you Mr. Razban."

Inspiration, at least to my limited understanding, results from us being human beings, and good human beings at that. The best way to be inspired is to be selfish. Be selfish enough to help yourself by helping others. To see someone else better off as a result of your words or your acts is extremely uplifting. One of my biggest sources of inspiration was when someone I'd helped find a job helped me get a job.

In a talk radio show, as a guest trying to help job seekers cope with sadness of jobless hopelessness, I shared my findings. "The best antidote to unemployment, underemployment, and unhappily employed depression is to inspire you is to keep busy!" When I go through those long unemployment cycles, I keep busy learning the latest developments in my career. I form teams with others, and help them while they help me or someone else to find a job."

Once you have plans for your future work life; once you see that you can be in control of your work life, then an empowering inspiration starts. This inspiration helps you discover almost unlimited stamina, power, and self-confidence that you did not even know you had.

That very same empowering inspiration must have been what made my chiropractor, Dr. Scott Cady one of the best of the best in his field. Based on several different indications, he is in top 5% among other professionals in his category.

As an experienced management consultant, I could sense this level of professionalism at work effectively in each and every visit to his office since 2005 when I became his patient.

In 2005, I suffered an excruciating foot pain that had made walking difficult. I had self medicated to reduce the pain but walking remained a constant problem. Finally the pain got to a point that it was not tolerable. When the pain gets to a point that we cannot take it anymore, we decide to do anything to sooth the pain. At that point, I was mentally ready for surgery, and pain killer shots like Cortisone.

About that time, I was referred to a surgeon who told me "I can fix your back pain problem by using a cadaver's spine disk to replace yours." I heard the word cadaver and I was out of his office just as fast as I could. The thought of a cadaver disk in my spine did not seem to set well with me in spite all the pain.

Hearing this, a good friend told me that he had a first class chiropractor. I limped and essentially pushed myself just as best I could to enter his office. After just a few treatments, my walking had improved a great deal.

Since this excellent result follows the same pattern as others, I decided to make a show case for best of the best practices in this book. His effective treatment had produced results and this is what makes the patients happy and keeps a business or practice successful. Dr. Cady is not working for a big company that is run by using other people's money. This practice is Dr. Cady's own money and his own business. As CEO of his life and career, he makes sure the best patient attention is paid to each and all patients at all times. His bedside manners make him an excellent person to trust and to work with.

Any money that is spent is actually his money. Any mistake that costs anything has to come out of his own pocket unlike others in big companies who are spending or managing other people's money.

Thus he is experiencing 90% efficiency in his practice while major corporations are experiencing about 70% or less. In fact many of my graduate students have told me that if there is any degree of dysfunctionality in major corporations, it can bring the real honest efficiency to about 30 to 40%. The rest is non-value-added waste of time, energy, and other resources combined with at best medium levels of customer and employee satisfaction.

In writing this book, I asked for an interview with Dr. Cady so we can have a candid discussion about what has made him so successful in his field. "Bruce, I followed my passion. Even today, after many years of practice, I know that I would chose this career anytime!" he told me. When asked why he chose to work for himself and not for a major corporation, he made the major point that "Working for yourself gives you freedom. Here I am free to have a vision; take calculated risks; lead, inspire, and empower myself and others so we can enjoy rewards. Of course, when my business decisions and risks do not pay off, I have nobody else to blame. I just quickly figure out what went wrong and take corrective action. There are no major prolonged business meetings or presentations. As a small business, I have to be agile and highly productive!"

I mentioned to Dr. Cady that I served the White House as a Silicon Valley leader in a bipartisan team of Democrats and Republicans in job creation. Then I added that several years after that assignment, which I took as an honor, I realized that the most effective way to create jobs is to use the good old American spirit of know-how and entrepreneurship. He seemed to be totally in agreement with this. "Entrepreneurs create jobs in small companies which are the backbone of our economy. Then these small companies grow and hire even more people. This is important! So, in addition to government doing their best in this area, we must empower and encourage the spirit of entrepreneurship to do its magic in creating jobs and wealth! They build businesses from nothing. They quickly learn that they have to be efficient to survive and succeed. They hire the right people, empower them, train them, and make sure they succeed since there is a very little margin of error in such companies." Dr. Cady has a big supporter of this idea in Sir Richard Branson who at the age of 14 started a record shop in London, and is now the President, CEO of Virgin Airlines. In fact, Sir Richard Branson in an interview in 2012 said "I would encourage the British government to give entrepreneurship loans to qualified students in addition to student loans!" Entrepreneurs, since they live in the business jungle that dictates the survival of the fittest, be customer-centric, learn to manage their money well, do things efficiently as well as being top notch professionals. "Bruce, I make sure that each and every patient is happy with me. I make sure that I explain to them what their treatment is about, and I take good care of them. This is not like some major clinic where the doctor has a few minutes to listen to the patients and make a diagnosis quickly and run to the next patient."

I asked him about how he defined job satisfaction since he was his own boss. "Bruce, ever since I graduated from Los Angeles College of Chiropractic, I have known that the best job satisfaction as well as the best job security for me is to see each and every patient who comes here get the best medical treatment that is the very best possible treatment that makes them happy. When I see a smile on their faces replacing pain, I know that I am very happy with my work. Well, at first when I started my business I had to be careful with money management, but now, as long as I make sure my patients are happy and well taken care of, I know that success and money will follow. There is no way that going for the patient satisfaction will not produce good financial rewards." Telling me this had convinced me that Dr. Cady must have studied Dale Carnegie as well the book that is titled, *"Do What You Like and Money Will Follow."* He was also proud to say that he has cultivated the same vision and attitude in most of the more than thirty interns that he has trained in conjunction with Palmer College of Chiropractic.

Then I asked him about his advice for young people who are entering this difficult job market. He started by quoting Walter Cronkite of CBS News who was honored as being the most trusted man in America. "Bruce there is no free lunch. If the new graduates cannot find jobs in their fields, they need to accept whatever they can get and not think that is below them." This was like music to my ears since he was talking about desperation jobs! Then he added, "You worked for Toyota as a car salesman during bad times and after making six figures income installing major IT systems for Toyota and Lexus when times were good." He also added that during the tough economic times, we all need to work harder and harder to succeed. He also pointed out the importance of making contacts with those who are successful in doing what we want to do in our careers and using them as role model.

"Bruce, I am not going to sugar coat this, we have to fight every step of the way these days that things are difficult and we live in turbulent times. But when you fight for what you believe in and what you want of your life and career, then the reward is so much sweeter. Oh, one other important thing, I advise young people to get an education in a field that is in demand and is closest to their own career and life passion. Remember that education in your primary field and other fields as well as what interests you is a lifelong effort."

Many years later after the 2005, when I arrived in his office after a major head-on collision, I could see his care and patience in getting all the information and making sure that he had spent enough time to make sure I understood all the facts and details regarding my injury as well as the treatment course.

This second go around was a complete validation and proof that he had maintained the same professional ethics and efficiency in treating patients the best way possible. Just like before he had determined what his core competence was and he would put it to use each and every day.

Over the years I have gotten outstanding results from him. When people are in charge of their own destiny, and are running their own business, they do successfully empower themselves to be the best of the best. He is indeed the CEO of his career and life!

I hope that by reading all my examples here, you can see that there is common thread that runs in the professional lives of all these CEOs of their careers and lives that is the same. The same set of principles works for doctors, professors, news casters, and anybody else who wants to succeed in business and their own professions.

This can also be true for you as the CEO of your own life.

Please Contact: bruce@razban.com

CHAPTER 14
Nobody can be a Better CEO for You than You!

My first professional job was in California, working for Plantronics. Those days, there was a Personnel Department. These days, they are called Human Resources or HR. The HR department had several employees who helped with hiring, salary administration, and career development, among other things. The career planning and development was what many companies did for their employees then.

When it was my turn to sit in a conference room to do my career planning with the HR representative I was elated. She had a chart that showed where I was as far as the title and job duties were concerned. Then she asked where I wanted to be in five years. The answer that was clear to me was totally puzzling to her. "I want to be a CEO someday!"

She politely asked, "So you want to go into management?"

Without any hesitation I proudly declared, "Yes Ma'am. I cannot wait to become a manager!"

She pulled out some paper that looked like cheat notes from college and carefully studied them for a minute or so. "Well then, you need to take some management seminars."

This was my turn to be puzzled. "Not really, I had a truckload of those courses in graduate school at the University of Wisconsin. I needed to become the best engineer to be promoted to management!" was my reply, based on what I had observed in the industry. The best engineers were usually promoted to managers, even if they had no people skills.

It took a few months before I was eventually convinced that management and technical are two different disciplines. To be a CEO someday, I needed to beef up my management skill set, which was quite different than the technical.

I was lucky that Jim Otts, a semi-retired former HP manager, took notice of me and became my mentor to prepare me for the art and science of management in daily practice. All the graduate classroom training could not compete with what I was learning from this mellow, competent, and professional engineering manager. He was like a professor during those fifteen minute coffee breaks as my mentor. Soon I was reading Dale Carnegie, and other inspiration books written by Dr. Wayne W.

Dyer. We would review my learning during those fifteen minutes each day.

Unfortunately, a lot of HR departments were severely downsized in the mid- and late eighties. Therefore, they did not really help with career planning. Nowadays, the successful people are those who are their own CEO and HR department for themselves. We have to care for ourselves; especially when there is nobody else to do this for us, as there used to be in HR departments.

I'm sure that you would be telling yourself that I'm asking for too much. I agree that this is too much to ask. Nevertheless, this is something that has become an absolutely needed part of working. If you suddenly lose your job, there is a chance that it will take you about one month for each $10,000 of the income that you used to make prior to the job loss. Days, weeks, months, and even years fly by; each week there is hope or hope that the last interview will actually get you the job that you prepared for so hard and interviewed well; then that job, along with several succeeding it, do not materialize. At this point, situational depression sets in; going to interviews starts to get more and more difficult; at this point you attempt to get advice from anyone who thinks they can give you advice to free you from your discouraging situation.

In my case, about fifty percent of the time my senior consulting or other employment came to an earlier finish; almost always they loved me and my work but there was a budget cut, downsizing, or off-shoring that cost me my job. Therefore, the statistics for many of us is that we had had to suffer unemployment or underemployment for about one and a half days for each day that we'd worked since 1996. The job search ordeal became a routine and frustrating part of our workday life. The same was true for executives from startups or major corporations, and permeated through all ranks. In my case, it was particularly painful, since I was getting age discrimination as well. I was doing the same disappointing job search as my colleague who had an MBA with twelve years of management, and a programmer friend did. I know a UC Berkeley Ph.D. who was gifted and internationally known as a computer scientist, who went without a paycheck for three years during this awful Global Financial Crisis.

The important point is that although it takes a bit more time to construct your own triple-decker career bus, that additional work is minuscule compared to pain, agony, and aggravation of having no jobs, or worse yet being stuck in underemployment or an awful that manages to devastate a bit of your existence every day.

We must be prepared for an eventual and sometimes inevitable sudden job loss. We must be proactively and continually active in the job search, or incorporation liberation, as explained in this book, whether we are unemployed or not! If we wait to start the job search until after we've lost our job, that's usually too late. Remember that constant vigilance is the price of freedom. To continue working in these turbulent times, we must be looking for potential new jobs all the time, and/or as the CEO of our own job and life, work on expanding our incorporation. I promise you that after a while job search becomes routine, and somewhat easy. I have yet to find somebody crazier than I who thinks job search is fun!

Here is suggested check list for constant job search:
- You have three sets of resumes for each of the triple-decker bus careers at the ready,
- You have a living document that is your career plan at the ready and reviewed by a few colleagues,
- You have a standby job(s) that you can jump on with short notice,
- Each day, you spend ten minutes doing your:

  - ✓ Networking about what's available and how they're doing, and offering to help them, but without asking them for a job then and there,
  - ✓ Review your job agents at several of the job boards as appropriate to your profession,
  - ✓ Review want ads in your newspaper and/or on Craigslist or eLance to be aware of what desperation job can be available to you if you were desperate enough to go for it.
  - ✓ Purchase a copy of the *Take this job and shove it* CD, or a DVD of *Most Horrible Boss* to give to your boss when he tells you, "You're fired!"
  - ✓ Did you know that you can fire your boss? You can do this when you are well and ready. Let me explain this, in 2008 market crash, American management got reinvented. This means that human intellectual property must be managed

with the same priority as materials.
Unfortunately materials management is all that our CEOs and managers are trained in managing. As such, either they learn, and learn quickly or they too are risking their jobs.

Having these things done helps you build confidence in the following ways,

- You do not have to put up with a horrible boss – by the way there was a movie by that title – or linger in a toxic work environment.
- You are now empowered; you can give the boss a taste of "at will" by resigning and going to a better job, or finding a job that is ideal, or a promotion, you will empower yourself to go do it.

Now you are in charge; you are not hopeless; you can be your own man/woman!

Even during the hardest of times, companies usually try to keep top talent, or people who are good at their work.

You might be thinking, "Bruce I am not a top talent! Being a top talent is much easier said than done. What are you talking about?"

The truth is that anyone can become a top talent in any well-defined and narrow skill-set. To do this one needs to have,

- A mentor. This is someone with more experience than you who has done what you are trying to do and has "walked the talk." In my case, this was Debra Benton, who is a New York Times best seller management and CEO book author.
- Constant improvement to your education. Colleges and seminars are the best way for this. I took one Java class in a commuter college that served me for many years to come.
- Advertise on Craigslist for "Tutor wanted," and spend $20 to $50 per hour to quickly come up to speed. I hope that Craig Newmar, the CEO, is proud of me for saying this. He is a champion and role model for us all. He, in a way, did the incorporation liberation.
- Now, let me add what I tell my clients as an executive coach, "Be willing to make mistakes, and, more important, learn from then on your way to almost sky-high success." My first book, *Layoffs and Hope* does have

more grammar and spelling errors than others because it was done on a shoestring budget and I did everything on my own. Most published books need fourteen people to do it right. However, it took seeing my first book on www.amazon.com to convince me that I have made it as an author.

The Global Financial Crisis of the 2008 and 2009 made it imperative that we need to act like the CEO of our work and life. We are now in command. Our career and work life is now our ship, and we need to act accordingly. When I first heard something like this, my reaction was that I just wanted to find my next job. I did not know that I had to act and think like a CEO to find my next job.

In Debra Benton's bio, one reads that she started by working for a company. Soon she found out that working for a paycheck from a company was not her dream. She felt like a renegade, and she became CEO of her own career. This empowerment has made it possible for her to thrive in her field.

Although I have a great deal of respect for many CEOs, and the fact that most of them are hard-working and competent, there are others who have room temperature IQ. Either they have blinding ambitions, or they are knowingly trying to pacify the short-term Wall Street profit motive, or they are just reckless and careless when it comes to employees' livelihood or customer's legitimate interests.

In these cases, this recklessness eventually backfires. It backfires because, as the number of laid off employees goes up, and as customer dissatisfaction mounts, it eventually takes its toll.

While there are cases where layoffs are indicated and a company has to do that for its survival, the layoffs and lack of management and leadership cannot be masked with "at will" hiring and firing, massive and frequent layoffs, and running a toxic work environment.

As a product engineer at Plantronics, inc. in Santa Cruz, I got the agreement of management to scrap about $3,000 worth of old parts. Managers did not have a good feeling about this. Some of us thought that those older parts could be refurbished and re-used. The test group was a bottleneck, since the refurbished parts needed additional tests. Finally, the management agreed that we needed to scrap these parts, since the labor cost for fixing and retesting would exceed the cost of buying the newer version.

I was trying to enjoy my cup of steaming coffee during my coffee break in my office when a foreman from the shop floor came up and knocked at my door. We had been on good terms, and talked freely about everything. "Bruce, we used to love you down there on the shop floor. But after the work order that scraps these $3,000 worth of parts, they're going to put the picture of your face on dart board and shoot darts at you!"

This really hurt. "Joe, I'm really sorry. As you know I am always honest with you. This was a painful decision for us to make too." I persuaded Joe to help me go over my analysis, promising him that if I was wrong I would correct it right away. We spent a good half an hour and went over the analysis step by step. I managed to convince Joe that the numbers would not tell lies. He hesitated for a moment, and then he carefully went downstairs only to rush up and take refuge in my office ten minutes later as if being followed.

"Joe, what happened?"

With a scared smile, he said that they would now put the picture of his face on the dart board!

It was near Christmas, and all of us were thinking about out profit-sharing check that Plantronics was always very generous and prompt in paying.

I got a call from one of my favorite assembly workers minutes later, saying, "Bruce, you know times are tough and we are counting on our profit sharing. So, let us volunteer to work on the parts free of charge. We'll work on them for free, if one of your engineers gives us a clear technical work order. Trust us, we will do it, and we will not throw darts at the picture of your face!"

Soon, Jim Otts, the former HPer who was my manager, offered to show up for work that Saturday and bring the chief designer along, too. The Director quickly announced that he'd bring donuts and coffee.

The refurbished parts were tested, and soon the production line was humming. Mutual trust and loyalty had done its job.

When the profit-sharing checks were ready to be distributed, our calculations indicated that each employee had $11.27 more to spend. However, a careful look at my check indicated that there was about $50 extra. The same was true with my manager's check. We informed the VP, and his response was, "Well, we decided not to collect our profit sharing as senior management, and we distributed it among others."

In the HP school of management, we call this teamwork and win-win!

That afternoon when checks were distributed, an employee brought her car, which had a fantastic audio system, and parked it right next to company yard, playing music and offering home-made Christmas cookies for all.

Dr. Stacy Quo is an excellent professional that my daughter has had the privilege of knowing.

Since her practice is her own, she makes sure tht everything is perfect for the patient. She is extremely nice and careful to all her patients who are teenagers for the most part.

As a senior management consultant, I could see that she had established a great deal of mutual trust and loyalty with my daughter and all other patients. She really cared since again this was her own business. Before and after pictures of her patients adorned her office along with a beautiful decoration of seashells and sands as if you were sitting near a beach.

She indeed is the CEO of her own career.

While her primary career is that of an orthodontist, she has also created and maintained a fantastic standby business to empower and strengthen her primary by being the personal business manager of the entire practice.

To make the point more clearly, every dollar spent or invested is coming out of her pocket and this motivates her and her staff to be efficient, patient, and business savvy as well as having the best equipment and best practices that the Internet can provide.

Watching her inspires me to go do the same and learn from her how to be the best of the best.

While one of her staff was taking an excellent care of my daughter's need, I noticed that Dr. Quo will go around and check each of the staff and in a positive way help them do things better and better. She was not micromanaging but she was enhancing the human capital and intellectual capital that she had in her loyal and professional staff and employees.

As in her case, being the CEO of her career has paid off handsomely. You cannot just go wrong with the idea.

Frequently when I ask my students about their job and life satisfaction as that applies to their jobs, I hear this, "Professor Razban 60 tom 65% of what we in the work place is a waste as it does not create any value add. A lot of money can be wasted as managers do not really care since it is not their own money.

One huge reward of being our own CEOs is the great deal of satisfaction it gives us in being the best of the best, have happy customers and employees and really make a difference for the better in this world.

Please Contact: bruce@razban.com

CHAPTER 15
What Does You Being a CEO Really Mean?

As my day-dreaming about becoming a CEO someday became more of an obsession rather than just a passing phase of my up-in-the-air career planning, I came across a book called *How to Think Like a CEO*, written by *New York Times* Best Selling Author Debra Benton.

This is a fascinating book that gives 22 invaluable insights and a comprehensive understanding of how a typical CEO operates.

- Sizes up themselves, others, and life,
- Becomes a CEO, and more important, how you can become a CEO too,
- Does what they do as a CEO

While it's true that this book was written for a corporate executive to learn how to become a CEO, it's also true that these days, after the Global Financial Crisis, we need to apply the same ideas to maintain our jobs.

Remember that about seventy percent of Americans and European employees are unhappy with their jobs. I'm totally ignoring self-serving statistics gathered by companies who asked their employees, "What is the level of your job satisfaction?" They might as well rephrase this as, "Tell us you are happy with your job so we won't fire you!" Then they might get the same 120% to 140% job satisfaction number to boast about. This is similar to the saying that everyone in Italy pays 120% of their income in taxes. By the way, this is a joke pointing out that some Italians, among other nationalities, under-report their taxable income. Thus they get the more than 100% figure of 120%.

Unlike a major corporation, when you become the CEO of yourself, you are an incorporation of one employee, which is one and the same as one CEO. And, this time, this is not some optional thing. To survive in the workplace of the future, you have no choice but to become your own CEO of your career and life.

Based on my firsthand experience, a CEO is in almost ultimate charge of the company. He or she is in charge and responsible for anything and everything.

Debra Benton's sizing-up idea can be done like this:

- As the CEO, I am in charge.

- As the CEO, I constantly need to take inventory of my skill set.
- As the CEO, I constantly need to refine and update my skill set.
- As the CEO, I need to have a roadmap on how to educate myself by a testable and virally marketable skill set. Remember, there is no one in the HR department to take care of this for you. It is you and you!
- As the CEO, I need to know what jobs are available out there.
- As the CEO, I need to do a good job of networking, even when I do have a job.
- As the CEO, I need to have my resume, references, and cover letter up to date and ready to go.
- As the CEO, I have to realize that I am a sales professional who needs to promote myself, as I am the corporation, the business, and the most important member.
- As a CEO, I need to have a strategic plan for myself. This includes what I want to be doing five years from now, and how to get there.
- As a CEO, I need to realize that there is no such a thing as job security any more.
- As a CEO, I need to realize that the best job security for me can be summarized in my skill-set, my ability to have friends and colleagues whom I can count on helping me get a job when I need one, and, according to *What Color is Your Parachute?* I need to learn what is new now, unlearn what was new before now, and to relearn what will be new tomorrow.

I was so touched by Debra Benton's book that I sent her a letter. To my pleasant surprise, the letter was responded to almost immediately. Debra was kind enough to personally respond. We exchanged emails, and I called her as soon as I got her phone number. Since then, she has been my most respected and encouraging mentor and role model.

I am now fully CEO of my own career and life. Because of the heavy empowerment I permitted myself to have as a CEO, I discovered that the most satisfying job for me is to be a writer, educator, and lecturer.

This was a major shift in the primary career part of my

jobs.

Unfortunately, the Global Financial Crisis has also meant that I, too, missed having a job for a while. These are difficult times for all!

Yet, I guarantee you that your day will also come as mine did. One balmy September day, my brother drove me to Fremont headquarters of Keller Graduate School of Management which is part of the DeVry University.

Soon during the interviews it became obvious to me and the two Deans that I was the right candidate for the university teaching.

My own empowerment in finding a job had paid handsomely. The mission for this job and my passion were one and the same. The work and play had now become one and the same for me.

As a result, I have gotten high student rating of my work and the job is so enjoyable for me that it makes me feel like I am flying in cloud nine all the time. When you love your work, the job becomes effortless and highly enjoyable.

My journey in writing this book has taken me from a cloudy day when I was trying to be a car salesman and in fact not being too good at it, to reporting to a CEO in a $500 million Dollar company. The highlight of the journey has been to be a senior management and technology consultant working at Simpson, Strong- Tie with an office right across the hallway from their outstanding C-Level executives including the CEO and also the founder Barclay Simpson's office.

Let me tell you a secret about management in general. Most of management is common sense. Also, an important part of management is proper application of the ideas that make us humans. It is no secret that as part of that being a senior management consultant at Simpson, I was using common sense and the basic management concepts and ideas that I was teaching in my graduate management classes.

This is so simple that it is mind-boggling.

Of course the idea here is that by becoming your own CEO, you find that you have proactive control over your career and even your life.

In a BBC interview with hostages who were kept in the worst of conditions. It became obvious that one of the important factors for their being able to cope, survive, and even succeed in their lives later on was to take control of their lives. This control could be in minor things. Nevertheless, this gave them a new meaning, a new outlook to things so they could just manage the terrible condition, the inhuman condition that they were left in.

Control is also the name of the game in hospital rooms. In these hospital rooms patients really have very little control over their medications and most of the treatment. However, some outstanding nurses have learned that the best way is to give any control, no matter how small so the patient feels better.

A nurse told me that by giving a choice to the patient on whether they want their medication right before 12:00 Noon, or right after that, patents tend to do better in taking the medicine. They tend to complain less even though the difference is only a few minutes.

How do we gain control?

The best way to gain control is to realize the following ideas:

- Have marketable and certifiable training from universities, colleges, and on the job.
- Be the best you can be by constantly networking with others who are in the field that you want to be.
- Make sure that you have a good life-career balance.
- Have a vision for what you want to be and where you want to be. This vision does not need to be perfect in every detail, but you must have a working sketch, a rough draft of how you and your work and life should look in three or six months or a year from now.
- Have a strategic which is a high level plan on how you make sure this happens.
- Have a detailed plan of what you plan to do each day, week, or month to achieve this plan. Make sure tht your results are observable and as realistic as they can be.
- Remember that education is an extremely important part of being your own CEO. Thus, try to get as much education as possible via universities, colleges, technical training organizations as well as making sure tht you get the latest and greatest from www.goolge.com, and www.youtube.com.

I fully understand that many of us are trying very hard to maintain even one career. I understand tht many of us work long hours at work and when we get home there is just a little time left to have some food and just simply pass out in front of the TV.

In fact this can be even more difficult when one is stuck in unemployment, underemployment or unhappy employment. Somehow the frustration and depression caused by these situations and especially in a toxic work environ takes all our control and desire away from us to succeed.

Unemployment in general is becoming a serious global disaster. The more we take matters at hand, the less chance that we will go without a job for a long time.

In an interview with KQED, Mr. Dirks who is the next president of the University of California, Berkeley pointed out that in general we will be migrating through six different careers in our lifetimes.

This is difficult to understand and to accept. For many of us our parents went to a college and university and got an education that lasted them a lifetime.

However, we see many people, including me, who had to migrate across many different boundaries to stay employed or to get out of a dead-end and disappointing job.

This makes good sense because:

- By having a triple-decker career bus you have more confidence and much better chances of getting employed.
- As one or more of the diversified career that you are in collapse or lose their ability to hire, you provide a seriously good cost benefit in a value-add fashion that companies will hire.
- Being CEO of your own career and life, gives you the chance to take those calculated risks needed to get ahead and succeed.
- Take full advantage of the American education excellence. We have still some of the best educational systems in the world. This is evidenced by seeing international students in almost all of our institutions of higher learning.

Learning is so important that there is now proof that most successful organizations are the ones that as an organization, the organization is capable of learning.

This can be done easier than it might look. A friend who was a successful computer professional always wanted to be a high school teacher. However, he had to have a certification for this and jobs were difficult to come by. So, he decided to be the CEO of his life and take matters at hand. He attended a special training seminar for high school teachers and even asked permission to go to some classes and be there just as an observer. Then, by networking he found out that one his best friends has been able to become a high school teacher. So my friend will invite that high school teacher to lunch and try to learn as much as possible from him during each lunch. This ended up with providing an excellent high school teaching opportunity.

An important factor in succeeding as being our own CEO is to learn to be an entrepreneur.

This is becoming more and more evident that in order to bring in business to our own company or as a consultant, we need to constantly promote ourselves and our company.

This fact was most evident in an interview with a Julliard school of music. Being accepted at Julliard, where only six percent of candidates are accepted, already points out that most students are outstanding.

In that interview with 60 Minutes TV program, Julliard officials were saying tht they encourage their students to constantly promote their own businesses.

For example, they were saying that in most cases their students do a great job in some performance and then they want to retire to their room to just relax.

The official was saying that he recommended to their students to go back to the audience and mingle with them as a way of promoting their potential concerts in the future.

Many authors like I, carry several copies of their books in the trunk of their cars so as to have them handing in case someone is interested in purchasing a copy.

One of my wife's friends had a small company that would provide chefs for restaurants. We invited to have dinner with us. She arrived with a shopping bag full of vegetables and other ingredients needed to cook an excellent dinner. We enjoyed that dinner that she had made as well as her way of explaining to us all the details on how and why she prepared that meal that special way. We could see that she was excited about this and she enjoyed every minute of it.

Soon we found out that she and two of her employees had found great jobs in a famous and outstanding restaurant.

One of my students decided to start a company that would compete with limousine services at a reasonable price. Soon he and his cofounder had purchased a second hand limousine and were offering their service to other students and their friends and families.

Unfortunately their business did not take off as they had intended. But they did not give up.

Last I heard was that they had started a successful business in doing the internet dispatching for several limousines.

Since I learned management from several HP employees (affectionately known as HPers), I have observed this company which was indeed one of the royalties of companies for many years and many reasons. Unfortunately there some recent years that has made HP somewhat less of an excellent company than it used to be. In my career of more than 30 years, nineteen years was spent working as a consultant for HP, working with HP on two alliances, and in fact in one case working for another company that was in some ways HP's competition.

Nevertheless, my best job ever still is the job that I had working for HP as a senior consultant in the www.hpshopping.com I was working in a division that reported to Carly Fiorina, the former CEO of HP.

It is interesting to note that I had and continue to have the highest for Carly. She in fact changed the DNA, which is even a stronger term for changing the HP culture.

Due to this, I usually play one of her most famous www.youtube.com clip in my graduate classes that are intended for graduating seniors. Carly speaks frankly about change, any change, creates fear. This is a strong emotional feeling that managers must be able to deal with before any change will ever happen. "Everybody is scared of something" she says and then she adds, "Organizations want to keep things the same. They do not like change!"

In many years of teaching I have learned that good managers work with this fear in a productive way by providing emotional and logical reasons that make the change a desired as opposed to being a fear.

On our parts, fear can and will become the prime setback if we do not take control of our careers and lives by planning and executing to fortify our own hob security by having the triple-decker bus fueled and running at all times!

Also by gaining control over our own destiny by acting as the CEO of our careers, we gain more self-confidence and more energy to put up a great fight instead of being scared and fearful about things.

Along with fear, lack of control can be an awful concoction for disaster. Lack of control can happen when you are having a good job as well as when you are unemployed.

Lack of control could happen if you are underemployed and know each day that your skill set in your primary career is eroding and you cannot or do not want to do anything to change this trend.

I experienced this awful concoction of fear and lack of control when my car was hit by another car that totaled my and the other person's car. When the airbag deployed I experienced a great deal of fear since this was the first time that this had happened to me. Soon the faint smell of gasoline added to fear while I realized that I had lost control over my car while it was skidding as the result of the severe impact.

Unfortunately, there is a third combination to this awful thing.

The third combination is loss of hope. Loss of hope brings in a powerful feeling of thinking nothing will work and what is the use of trying. We have seen this clearly in the case of many unemployed people who lose hope so bad that they do not even try to find a job.

In almost all cases when people lose their jobs, they internalize it. They tell themselves that they most have done something that they should have not done, or did not something that they had had to do. And then they get fixated in this state of hopelessness for a long time.

This hopelessness then ties handsomely into a great justification for thinking that they do not have control and then that is the time when fear takes out all their energy and happiness.

I know a woman who had a PhD from one of the best universities in the world and who spoke four languages and who was an excellent pioneer for ADA programming language that was meant to be the most important language to the entire US military.

Suddenly she lost her job.

Some years later she told me that she even gave up looking for a job. Then she continued that "As time went by and as I was sinking more and more in my depression that was caused by fear, hopelessness, and lack of control, the door bell rang. Reluctantly, I opened the door to see the door man. He had a letter that contained and excellent job opportunity. I got the job and a few months later the entire hopelessness, fear, and lack of control had gone away."

I have seen the same happen to me. One day, I am down and depressed for not having a consulting gig and a few weeks after starting to work, I am back to my jovial self again.

Thus there is great reward to proactively do the best we can to be CEO of our lives and careers one day at a time, one hour at a time, and even one minute at a time.

Please Contact: bruce@razban.com

CHAPTER 16
What a CEO will do in the Workplace of the Future?

If you decide to be a one person company or a small business, the CEO will have to be you. Since this is your own business, your own pocketbook, and your own future, chances are that you will do great.

This is a good time to bring the "Triple-Decker Career Bus" concept into focus.

There is a proverb that says a man needs a wife who cleans, cooks, takes care of his emotional needs, and finally loves him. The punch line is, "That this means three wives!" Another way of saying this is that a woman needs a husband who loves her, is sensitive, and is caring. The punch line here is that a woman needs three husbands. This is triple redundancy to make sure one does not fail.

Why I am telling this stupid joke? The reason if any escapes me.

Many business owners, and especially independent consultants, have learned that they need to diversify. This has meant that they need to have three careers. In other words have multiple choices and diversified careers in marketable and certifiable areas.

The main part of the career is what most of us have had. I, for an example, consider my primary career as being a manager.

In lean times like these, it might become important that I have diversified so I can survive. For example, when I worked for Plantronics, I did my primary career of management of some sort.

Then, there are steady and always waiting job(s) that you have to develop, even though you have a job. For me, this has meant learning to sell cars, and/or work on automotive IT systems. As you know, most everything is computerized these days. So, when things got really bad, I ended up going back to Toyota Sunnyvale and asking for a job there. This put bread on my table for two months, even though the wage – which is heavily commission-based – was a few percentage points below my unemployment check. I was not as good as their top Internet saleswoman, who sold twenty cars a month.

Please note that having this standby job required that I stopped by and visited from time to time. It required networking with my colleagues from time to time. I kept in touch with them, even when I did not need a job right away, and did them some favors. For example, I got a Lexus baseball cap for one of the Toyota salesmen so he could boast to others that he drove an expensive Lexus and not that beat up 18 year old truck.

I have a good friend in the Lexus dealership. Being the CEO of a particular dealership, he has been twice able to get me a job during the down times. However, this, too, has required monthly contacts and in one case stopping by at 7:00 AM with some steaming Crispy Cream donuts for the repair department. I also brought fresh containers of Starbucks coffee.

You have to keep these relationships alive when you don't need them so they will be there when you *do* need them. There are ongoing benefits, as well. For example, when the window up/down switch broke in my Lexus, due to some minor accident, my buddies at Lexus took care of me. The repair department made one phone call to his old friend in a Chicago junk yard, and I had the part delivered to me by FedEx overnight, for $12.50. Incidentally the overnight FedEx charge of $18 or so was really needed, since I couldn't close the window and it was the rainy season.

My experience shows that we do not do business, we build relationships. It is these relationships that come to the rescue us when we have to get a job.

Going back to that triple redundant, triple-decker bus, this was the example of the second floor, which was the standby job. This is a job to be had when things get bad. Remember that this job is not as good as your main career job. Hopefully, it will pay the bills.

The final level is the top floor.

This is called desperation jobs. This is when a Ph.D. friend of mine became a cab driver in New York City. This is when I got a job, the only job that I could get during the dot-com bust, which was working 35 hours a week in a retail shop, mainly selling electronic parts. I had not cultivated this job. I didn't even know that such job existed beforehand. However, it really saved the day for me. But I was willing to take any job so as to have something to do. In fact sometimes being unemployed and having nothing to do is so painful and boring that we are even willing to pay someone money just to work for them instead of them paying us.

The title being desperation jobs might in fact be harsher than it should be. Perhaps this category of jobs should be called "less than ideal" jobs. However, the main benefit of these jobs is that one feels productive and puts some bread on the table. It also keeps people in circulation and keeps their psyche in a good shape. In comparison, sitting at home and feeling sad and remorseful is the other alternative when jobs are difficult to find.

Finding a desperation job is an excellent way to avoid being unemployed for a long time or even for a short time and it really helps. Many of us who try this route find that no honest job can be beneath us, and more importantly any job even a desperation job can add to our skill set portfolio.

In a Sunday afternoon, I was attending my Click University, Googeling around, and URL surfing when I came across an article that said "Norwegian PM Jens Stoltenberg spent an afternoon incognito as a taxi driver in Oslo, he had revealed. He said that he wanted to hear from real Norwegian voters and that taxis were one of the few places where people shared their true views. The stunt was organized by his Labor party and the footage will be used as part of his campaign for re-election in September."

I know quite a few people who were much better off regarding their personality and skill sets after they spend some time doing a desperation job. A friend told me that his interpersonal skills have improved 200% after he had to go back to being a bartender in New York City after many years of being an account manager helping people with tax audits. In another case, a high level computer architect from a reputable Silicon Valley company who had become a security agent in San Francisco Airport decided not to go back to his old job even when things had gotten much better and his old company was begging him to go back. He loved his family time much too much to go back to that sixty hour a week regiment that was routine in his old job. His desperation job that now had become his permanent job was forty hours a week by being ten hours a day for four days. Then, he had a three day weekend every week that he would spend with his family and friends.

I have also seen people in a desperation job who re-invented themselves and their careers by "re-tooling" their skill set or doing heavy connection enhancements that would then get them a good standby job on their way to going back to their primary jobs.

I call this 1-2-3 punch! First you find that you are stuck and either there no jobs or you cannot or do not want to find a job. So, you find a job which pays a lot less than what you are used to by answering to a help wanted sign in a store window nearby. Secondly, as a result of this you see that you meet many others while doing your job. One day you meet someone who can help you get back to your original primary job or another primary job that fits your newly acquired skill set even better. Thirdly, after a hiatus, you got back with your batteries charged and your spirit high to that or other primary job. I have also seen that the desperation job had shown some people how to become better in an old or new hobby. Also, I have seen some people decide that they would love to volunteer some or all of their jobs doing charity or other community work; I have seen people get involved more with their kid's school that really needed their help really bad.

I guess what we are learning here is that we no longer can rely and rely only on one career and one time school. What we are seeing is that we must have a 3-in-1 career which is symbolized with the triple-decker bus in this book. This is in sharp contrast to the old days that one got a four or more years college degree and education phase of life was done with. Then there was the second phase of getting a job that lasted until they retired. This also seems to be a thing of the past. Thus we arrive at the age of life-long Internet education, quick on-the-job training, and constant search for the next full time or part time job in case of sudden job loss.

We need to be continuously caring and feeding all three; the main career, the standby, and desperation job. We need to do this whether we have a job or not. What we do not want to happen is be caught without a job for any extended period of time.

Please Contact: bruce@razban.com

CHAPTER 17
Greed, for the Lack of a Better Word, is Good!

As of this writing, the average forty-three-year-old American has no more than $45,000 in his or her IRA account. According to CNN reports, the average American has nine credit cards. So, considering that the average cost of living for an American family of three or four is somewhere between $6,000 to $8,000 per month, and assuming no unexpected events like sickness or hefty car repairs, the average American can "retire" for just seven months.

And, the average American has minimal savings. The sad thing is that, for many of us, we are only fifteen or so paychecks away from becoming homeless!

This was one cold, hard fact that I did not understand, or did not want to understand, all the years that I was gainfully employed.

The invisible man, who is a homeless fellow in the Streets of San Francisco, was instrumental in my awakening to this fact. The fact was that I, too, was about fifteen paychecks away from being homeless, just like him. This was a shock for me to comprehend.

This explains why I talk about this subject in this book. This is dear to my heart.

But the invisible man was a title he had granted himself, since a lot of people ignored him when they walked past him, as if he was indeed invisible.

The invisible man seemed to be in his twenties, he was usually clean, and he would hold his sports cap in front of passersby and ask for money. He seemed to have a style of his own, as well as considerable self-respect.

I usually saw him during the lunch hour, and I usually had a dollar bill folded to drop in his cap. He would usually say, "Thanks young man," (even though I was fifty-eight at the time, and looked it). I would say, "Thanks for the undeserved complement!"

Then we would have a minute or so of conversation on many subjects, including arts, careers, airlines, family life, Madonna, the Iraq War, the economy, computers, utility companies, and even psychology. He was clearly able to carry on a conversation at the level of a college graduate who was reading the

San Francisco Chronicle almost every day.

Sometimes, I wondered if he, with his wasted knowledge, could maybe make a good, or at least average, elected official of the government, if only he had the resources available to him.

What a waste for this man to live on $20 to $25/day on a good day, and only $3 to $4 on a bad day. Rainy days in San Francisco—this most beautiful and sophisticated bride of a city—were particularly depressing to him since tht meant he would make very little money.

One day he told me about an article in his paper that he was sure was from the *New York Times*. The article said that the average working American was only fifteen paychecks away from homelessness. It certainly was true about me, a senior consultant with more than thirty years of experience and in one of the most lucrative fields, high tech in Silicon Valley, California.

When I worked for PG&E in the San Francisco Financial District, I would see several homeless people near where I worked. Some were victims of some sort of mental disease, and there were some that just did not look the part of the typical homeless. Among those, I found a college student who was reading a highly intellectual book and seemed to have fairly decent clothes. When I dropped some coins in his cup and started a conversation, he told me that he was a member of the *fresh* homeless. His mother had just kicked him out of her house and asked him to go get a job.

By the way, I have other heroes. There is a man who lost everything he had about three months after he lost his job. I think he was a pipefitter for new buildings. Being single, he decided to take his beat up truck and tiny trailer and move to another area that was not so badly hit. For about two months, he "lived" in that tiny space during his off hours from working in a donut shop. Right after his shift was over in the donut shop, he would walk two blocks to work somewhere else.

He worked as hard as he could each day, and at night he would pass out in that trailer.

I saw him every morning when I went to get my breakfast. In spite all this hardship, he was proud, and one time I heard him boast to another worker that he had saved about three hundred.

Just like this man, we have a great number of invisible unemployed or underemployed people whose talents and productivity is wasted, yet they are not part of our unemployment statistics.

That is the sad part. If some CEO or venture capitalist gives my blueprint a chance, I can prove that we can avoid this waste and put it to good use. We're doing something like this in hybrid cars. When you press on the brake, the energy that used to go waste can now be stored to be used next time you press on the gas pedal. Let's use the same concept with a 107.8% employment. Let's help our workers stay globally competitive, let's do what the old Personnel Offices or Human Resources Departments used to do, and cannot do today. Let's be greedy capitalists who want to make money, and lots of it! To do this, we need to focus on and empower our human capital. This is so easy and simple that it defies imagination, since we are brain-washed to think that 4% Unemployment is ideal. Yet this "ideal" 4% unemployment is responsible for a $2.4 Trillion productivity loss each year.

Let's stop our addiction to layoffs!

This makes it enough of talking about layoffs and their negative effect. Let me tell you something interesting. Careers as well as life sometimes have setbacks and mistakes and just plain failure. To prevent the impact of these things companies, organizations, and individuals proactively plan and work on reinventing themselves. In fact, if you look at HP logo it used to have the reinvent as part of it.

To remain competitive, many companies and people reinvent themselves. One of my best students was a successful director in a company and yet he was not happy with being a manager. He wanted to go back to being an engineer. The problem was that there had been many years since he had been doing any engineering work. So, he started taking classes in network security at night at a nearby college. Soon he had the certificate and he was able to convince the CEO of his company that he could be of much more benefit to the company as a programmer than a director.

After a mutually agreed transition, he was extremely happy as a senior programmer and the company had benefited for exchanging one unhappy and ineffective director and transforming him into a super programmer.

As a proud American Capitalist I am glad to tell you that the Global Financial Crisis has also transformed Capitalism by forcing it to put just as much emphasis on intellectual capital as it did on material capital and move at the speed of light which is what Internet demands these days.

Soon you will see many companies and even local businesses fail when they do not reinvent themselves to be productive in the era of the reinvented Capitalism.

You will see mass unemployment in many countries that is around 20 to 50%; you will see the fabric of societies break as a result of this massive and global unemployment; and you will see monumental success of people, organizations, and companies that adhere and prosper by using this reinvented Capitalism.

An important note is made here to keep things straight. Capitalism, even the old one, was superior to other forms of economies. One reason is that many older countries like China, Russia, and others have embraced Capitalism and entrepreneurship in some form or the other after their old system was failing.

Let us continue talking about greed. I respect the fact that Capitalism understands human nature that people are greedy. The more we have the more we want. Unfortunately, the entire science of economics tells us that world's material properties are scarce. There just is not enough of all the material things that we like to consume and consequently even waste.

In fact according to Peter Senge, a highly respected MIT management professor and consultant, we are already using, consuming, and wasting 1 ½ times as much material resources that planet earth is able to provide. His prediction is that as India and China fully get to take advantage of their newly gained wealth, then we will in a few years new 3 times as much resources as the planet earth can provide.

Now, let us contrast materials capital against human intellectual capital.

Wow! Unlike material capital that the more we consume, the less we have left, in the case of intellectual capital, the more we spend the more we can generate and the more we have. This comes from the fact that human capability to innovate, renovate, and re-invent is just limitless. To those who are sentimental, human capital is just like love since to romantic people the more lovers you give the more you have left.

This is a great match for the understandable human nature of greed. Remember that the more we have, it is natural to want more.

As we learn new things in this age of digital humanity, we will be able to use the Internet and all the other technologies to not only invent gadgets, but also to produce more of human intellectual property capital that can solve not just gadgetry needs but also human needs.

Now in this new capitalism, let us put greed to use. Let us say to our scientists that we will pay them same amount money as our athletes make if they produced gadgets that were designed to solve human needs.

This is precisely what Bill Gates or Microsoft is doing. He is trying the same technology that made laptops that said "Intel Inside" to save potentially millions of lives in Africa with his generous high tech products.

The learning here is that as CEO of your career and life, you might want to put your own greed to work and create devices that sure we can irradiate world hunger, childhood diseases, and many other things that have shamefully beleaguered our world.

This explains well other thing that I have been talking about. To make money, and make a lot of it, your focus will need to be on philanthropic profit-making. In other words instead of using the old materials-based only Capitalism that focused on profits at any cost, try to look at how best we can serve this digital humanity and you will make a lot more profit than the other way.

Let us look at Google business logic which is fundamentally designed to do no harm. The entire world uses their free service which is a humanitarian and philanthropic thing. Yet they are making a lot of money using the philanthropic profit making concepts.

Predicting what the key success will be in 2014, Carly Fiorina, former CEO of HP pointed that in the earlier years companies believed that as HP did too that they needed to do business and not do harm. However, she thinks that in the future it should be "Doing well and doing good." That be done by innovation, training, and development of the human capital.

Please Contact: bruce@razban.com

CHAPTER 18
Vicious Cycles of the Past

As you saw in previous chapters, the owners were the ones who managed the business in the past. This is true today about many small businesses, and it might well be the reason why small businesses are the highest job providers and the backbone of American economy. In these companies, every decision directly impacts the owner's pocket. The owner, who is acting as the manager, is directly responsible and accountable to herself. Not only that, but the owners are usually in close contact with their customers and employees. As such, they have the effective and powerful feedback mechanism of hearing from their customers and employees when they make a bad decision. This will make a company act more along the lines of developing and maintaining a good information flow and a good level of mutual trust and loyalty.

However, as companies got bigger and bigger, this umbilical cord that maintained information flow and mutual trust and loyalty was chopped off!

In general, many CEOs of big corporations were secluded and isolated from their employees and customers. They would spend as much as sixty or even seventy percent of their time absorbed in some colorful Microsoft PowerPoint presentation that was filtered by many levels of management, stockholders, and even short-sighted Wall Street. I've witnessed many of these presentations to C-level executives. I've realized how distorted and distant a pretty and colorful image on the projection screen can be from the grim and painful reality that is crystal-clear to each and every employee and customer. After being in business for more than thirty years, I can sense and mentally see the really grim picture, regardless of all the colorful presentations.

In many companies, layoffs are not just a one-time thing! However, layoffs do not work in the long term. Many companies are relying on frequent and massive layoffs just to operate. Unfortunately, the consequences of layoffs eventually destroy companies, careers, and even lives.

In the *Kabala*, one of the Jewish holy books, it says that everything is connected to everything else. Based on this, and the fact that with global markets the entire world is connected to each other, vicious cycles resulting from layoffs can have global consequences.

Consider this:

Event 1: A company experiences low sales and/or low revenue.

Event 2: The Company decides to cut costs. This is based on the false assumption that cutting the work force results in savings. This is a knee jerk reaction instead of trying to increase sales, empowering employees, or even understanding what really caused the problem.

Event 3: The Company decides to lay off employees.

Event 4: Morale goes down, and resources to do the job, or to do it right, are not there anymore!

Event 5: To cope with Event 4, the company decides to cut services and skimp on quality.

Event 6: Customer expectations are not met. The Customer Satisfaction Index goes down.

Event 7: Surprise, surprise, customers DO NOT BUY.

Event 8: Customers DO NOT BUY results in low sales and/or revenue!

Event 9: As President Regan said, here we go again! Back to Event 1!

Many companies who do repeated layoffs end up going out of business, or are acquired by another company. The layoff thing does not work in the long term. Layoffs destroy creativity. They destroy the fragile yet vital mutual trust and loyalty among employees, between the employees and management, and this severely affects the ability of a company to produce good products and services.

One devastating fact is that excellent employees decide that they do not have to put up with constant fear of the next layoff, and they find another job and leave. On the other hand, those employees who are not the best, or feel that their skills are marginal, get scared and start looking for another job elsewhere. They leave, too.

Then, companies which by now are desperate to get things done pile the job of two or three employees on a poor survivor employee. Tempers get short. Conflicts among employees become more severe, more frequent, and more damaging. To save their jobs, employees end up playing more politics and games. This happens at the expense of productivity and creativity.

With this much turmoil, customers do not get their money's worth. As we said, since everything is related to everything else, when customers are not satisfied with one company, they go to the competition. The company that laid off employees loses, and employees and customers lose too. *Everybody* loses in a layoff! The entire company becomes victim to low morale, politics, and trying to save jobs at any price.

The "at will" employment regulation, which says that the company can fire, and the employee can quit, at any time, has had an awful impact on productivity, and mutual trust and loyalty. The "I do not care, you do not care, and attitude on the side of companies, employees, and customers" that prevails is the destructive side of this layoff frenzy.

During a recent lunch at a national fast food restaurant, I noticed that about thirty percent of their employees were not there compared to previous times I went there. Unlike previous times, the food was cold by the time it got to our table, and it was more salty than before. After the recent layoff, three people had to do the job of four or five.

This was yet another demonstration of the futility of layoffs and their damaging impact on businesses and human beings that form the company.

In contrast, let's look at an icon of the restaurant business. Chez Pannisse has been doing brisk business, and benefitting from high respect and praise for many decades, in Berkeley, California. In an interview with Terry Grosse of the *Fresh Air* program, the owner said, "We are in the business of building a relationship with our customers, vendors, and employees. We want this relationship to be one of mutual trust and loyalty! Since we need to have the freshest ingredients each and every day, we hold ourselves responsible for making sure that our vendors are provided for. This creates a long term effective and profitable mutual dependence. The vendor cares, and thus gives us high quality vegetables. If there is a problem, we do not hide it or blame each other for it. We work together to solve it!"

Let's go back to the fast food example. The company does not care if the product and service is of high quality. In addition, the company does not care for the employee's morale or career. The employee does not care for the company's customers and their experience.

    In contrast to this, I would like to tell you about Original Joe's. For more than fifteen years, my family and I have been going to this restaurant for exceptionally great food and service, at reasonable prices. This is a genuine Italian and genuine American restaurant and bar. Every time that we go there, this restaurant proves to us that we can have our cake and eat it too!

    The reason I say this is that we get gourmet quality food served professionally and well and by people who care. This excellent food and service is not pricey. We have always had an excellent dining experience there, and were never disappointed.

    For years, I've had their world-class steak and eggs for breakfast, "De-li-ciouso!" spaghetti or chicken parmesan for lunch; and many different entrees for a complete dinner. In addition, they have been my favorite, and many other managers', place to go for business lunches and dinners. Since they are located within walking distance of hotels and conference centers in downtown San Jose, it's almost automatic for us to end up there for a nice breakfast, lunch, or dinner, or just a few drinks with clients to discuss business matters in a relaxed environment. This was so much so that while attending a conference in a nearby hotel which even provided free lunch, several colleagues and I pretended to enjoy the food from a famous restaurant only to sneak out early and go have our excellent food at Original Joe's.

    A lot of wining and dining that used to take place during up markets has gone away in this bad economy.

    The last time I was there was a Monday. As I mentioned, this restaurant is in walking distance of many places in San Jose. That morning, I was interviewing people as part of writing this book. My impromptu interview that day was with a young couple near the bankruptcy court at 280 South 1st street.

    "We are sick and tired! We just lost everything we worked for all these years. And the bill collectors keep calling us day and night; they do not leave any messages, and when we do pick up after the many calls they make each day, they do nothing but harassment. This major credit company knows, and we know that this is unethical and illegal, but they do not care!" Was the first thing I heard from this couple.

Just to have some privacy from a person standing next to them who seem to be eavesdropping, they told me in perfect French that they were finished. They told me that they feel so much shame for having to do a Chapter 13 bankruptcy after several years of running the business to the best of their capabilities. I took some mental notes and was ready to thank them and leave when the man who seemed to be eavesdropping almost begged me to hear his story.

His story was just as heartbreaking and discouraging as that of the younger couple. "Mr. Razban, I worked for the government. I put up with some boring job that was driving me crazy; when I tried to get something done in a reasonable time, I would be warned by my co-workers that I should not do it that fast. Their reasoning was simple. If someone worked fast and got the job done well, others would be expected to do the same."

Then, to continue to have my attention, he said that he was the victim of a layoff. I told him that I had envied a secure and sit-back government job for many years, even though they did not pay well.

Upon hearing this, he went into a serious protest. "Mr. Razban, you wasted your life being jealous of me and my government job! My job was a dead end job. There was little chance of ever making it big; we were never paid as much as in the private sector; we could never dream and dream big like you guys did with startups of Silicon Valley; we could not even imagine a chance of striking it rich quick; we could not even try to do a www.google.com, or www.amazon.com, even if we had the perfect idea and were willing to work extremely hard at it. We were just like millions of other government workers elsewhere on this globe, minding our seniority at the job and thinking about not rocking the boat!"

I started to try to gently reason with him that I am a proud American; this is my country, good or bad; and I still think that I should have had a stable government job to avoid all the rollercoaster job rides that I'd had.

With visible anger igniting in his voice and body language, he emphatically added, "And Mr. Razban, the so-called job security is not there anymore, either! I was let go due to a budget deficit. All that work and showing up each day to keep our seniority, and then suddenly we were on the sidewalk, just like others from the private sector. Did we not? I challenge you; look at me declaring Chapter 7 bankruptcy today! At least this couple tried their life's dream; at least they had the guts to do what they wanted! Did they not?"

Just like a kid who is told there is no Santa Claus, I walked from this office, which was in a government facility, to the parking lot where I had parked my car. The insanely heartless machine near the exit demanded a $14.00 parking fee. Now I knew that I had totally lost my sanity as I started to argue with the machine. Without hearing a word I had said, the machine blinked the $14.00 in blood red digital LEDs and in less than ten seconds, as if it will be calling the cops on me, started to let out some screeching and irritating combination of beeping and alarm!

After a few minutes of driving, and somewhat upset, I decided to treat myself to Original Joe's excellent dining to sooth my anger and frustration. My day, which had started pretty badly, seem to turn a bit luckier as I approached my favorite restaurant. The parking spot right near the entrance door of the establishment was empty, and the meter even had twenty-four minutes left on it.

As soon as I entered, the cashier noticed that I was walking with a limp. "Sir, I will get you a place very close so you do not have to walk much."

I was happy to see someone good at their job and really caring. I started to be spoiled a bit and asked, "Can I have a booth that is close and yet quiet? I need to chill out after having had a difficult day so far!"

She responded quickly, "Of course, I understand, Sir. Can you please walk five steps more and I get you one of the quietest booths!" Just to make sure, she asked, "Is this table OK for you?"

Seconds after I sat down, the general manager handed me the menu and asked if I was ready to order a drink while I was reading the menu. Then he introduced the waiter who had been there for many years.

This prompt, yet professional, treatment encouraged me to ask if I could have only half of the pasta. "Yes sir, we have this three quarter option on the menu where you save $4.00 by ordering less pasta." Then I asked them to prepare the pasta just the way I wanted it and asked to have a meatball on the side as extra. The food was prepared and presented even better than I had ordered it. I was not surprised, because the waiter had listened carefully and even suggested several other options, and had confidentially made sure that he knew exactly what I wanted. The food was on my table by almost exactly the time that the waiter told me.

Since I was writing this book, I asked if I could see the manager. The general manager came, and I told him that I was writing a management book and I wondered if I could ask a few questions. He answered all my questions thoughtfully, and then waved to the owner to come join us, if it was OK with me. The owner seemed to be well-educated and extremely competent as a manager. He was polite, and after carefully studying my questions would offer his point of view.

"What makes you such a successful institution after all these years? What helps you stay in business when several of your competitions have gone out of business all around you? What's your secret, if you can tell me?"

Carefully choosing his words and with a confident smile he told me that there was no secret. He told me that,

- We hire our employees carefully, for the long term, and we are always there to help them provide a better service for the customer,
- We feel a strong obligation to serve our customers well and make sure that they are happy with us each time they come here,
- Our best advertising is word of mouth,
- Over the years, we have established a good customer base, like yourself, and we will never disappoint them; we try to earn their business each and every time as if it was the first time they came here; we try to build a strong relationship with them, and not just serve a meal or two and maximize our profits just on that,
- We are very careful with menu prices,
- Our suppliers know us and we've know them for many, many years. We do right by them, and they do right by us. This was extremely similar to what I heard about the Chez Pannisse restaurant at Berkeley,
- We are committed to each and every customer, employee, and supplier. Our customers and employees are our responsibility, as if they are our relatives. We give them value for their money.

111

He was telling me about HP-Way (without knowing this management concept, but practicing it, as it was good for the business). He was telling me that he enjoyed doing a good job, and took pride in it.

For a moment, I thought that maybe these guys have been lucky all these years; maybe somehow they were immune to this bad economy. My barrage of questions that were coming like a military interrogation continued. However, I noticed that I did not stop him from convincing me that he knew all about these tough times. He knew that his two boys might have a lower standard of living than him. "On Father's day, I went to check two of my closest competitors and their business. In one restaurant, there were four waiters and only two customers; in another one, there were six customers and five waiters. This tells me how bad the economy must be. We, on the other hand had our usual number of steady customers dining with us on that Father's Day, just like all previous years. Having said this, we do sense that it is more and more difficult for our customers to dig into their purses or wallets to pay the check, even though, unlike many other restaurants, we have not increased our prices that much."

He had been resigned to the fact that the American economy and businesses were in crisis. Nevertheless, he was there to serve his customers best way he knew how, each and every day.

In the middle of our discussion, the waiter, trying not to interrupt our discussion, said, "Sorry sir, I am afraid your food has gone cold. Would you like me to warm it up?" He soon was back with a cold glass of Coke, anticipating my next request. Interestingly enough, my exciting discussion with the owner had necessitated another request for heating up the food again and the waiter had it done cheerfully.

As I left the restaurant, I felt like I had just gone to one of the best restaurants in New York City. Living in Manhattan for almost a year, I had become quite a restaurant snob! However, I was so impressed with the royal treatment at Original Joe's that I decided to make this place a showcase in this book. Showcase, not just because of the great food and service and reasonable prices, but primarily from superb management.

Poor management was what got us into this Global Financial Crisis, and good management is what gets us out of it.

I talked to the owner about his ambitions. His response was, "If there were less business taxes and regulations, I would like to franchise Original Joe's. With less regulations, overhead, and red tape, and if the economy gets better, I will hire. But, not right now, since there is just too much uncertainty. Yeah, as a small business owner, I am determined to do what I can to help by hiring. Unfortunately, it looks like I will not be hiring in the foreseeable future."

We talked about my book a bit more. Then it was time for me to go to my next interview meeting for this book, with an Indian-American executive friend of more than thirty years.

After an extended discussion of economy and the fact that as a co-founder of a startup company in Silicon Valley he has had no paychecks in eight months, we decided to have a drink and talk about politics.

As you might have imagined, the rapid economic growth in India and China has made these countries rivals. "Bruce, let me tell you, as an American citizen, that America is already a third world country. The Chinese will be consuming more energy than us. I think what the Chinese government likes to see is that we pay our bills. They will soon make it clear to us that we have to become subservient to them and stop all this nonsense about American freedom! They want to make us understand that we are no longer their boss, but that they are the boss of us!"

As for his own country of origin, India, his reaction was that there is much too much corruption, and there is serious lack of the infrastructure needed for them to sustain such astronomical growth forever.

Then, in a burst of good news he said, "Man! I still have faith in America. Look, we rebuilt Europe after the war; we still pay plenty of support to too many countries! We are still the symbol of global freedom – unlike the Chinese – and they want us to do the same! I do not recommend us to become the police of the world. However, we have a role, almost a divine role, to lead, empower, and free the world. We like to see India as a free and democratic world just like ourselves."

That afternoon, thanks to Skype, I was talking and looking eye-to-eye with my friend of many years who used to teach at prestigious London School of Economics. "Mr. Razban, I think that this is going to be a difficult time for all of us, for a long time. Since I live in Europe, I can explain that the problem in Europe is that the Greek and Portuguese economies are bringing down everyone else in Europe. Maybe the Euro-Zone needs to be abandoned; maybe we need to ask Greece and Portugal to stay out of the EU for a while until things get better." He seemed to think that America was better off than Europe, when it comes to banking, at least.

The very next day, having coffee with the former CEO of a computer corporation, he told me, "Bruce, the way for capitalism to succeed is to let some companies die. When companies become too big for their own good, and especially when they become complacent and top-heavy, the natural market forces should let them fail, so new smarter and more agile small companies take over the market share."

In my thinking, the economy is not like the weather, which we have absolutely no control over. I'm convinced, after these thirty years, that we must manage the economy and business.

Management is totally different than controls. I believe in the free market. However, imagine that everyone was free to go to the airport any time they wanted; airlines were free to fly in any navigational pattern they wanted; companies were able to charge anything they wanted and run their business exactly the way they wanted! That would not be free market. It would be complete anarchy and chaos. We must have some sort of self-appointed management to make sure things are not going wrong.

During the last thirty years, I have seen the same human and management behavior and company processes that have created bubbles and then killed them more than four times. It is so similar that it's like watching the re-run of a previous re-run of a boring show. As Yogi Berra used to say, this is déjà vu all over again, in a nightmarish pattern.

In a NOVA program called *Mind over Money*, broadcast by Public TV, an interesting case was given for the painful repeated bubbles rising and bursting. According to this program, the first bubble was created and burst in Holland. There was a thriving and hot passion for tulip bulbs that would make some of them worth even more than a house. The prices skyrocketed, until on February fifth, 1637, the bubble burst and many people were out of their money. Just like the financial crisis now. The same déjà vu happened all over again in October 1929, were the market crashed. At that time, 9,000 banks failed; there was 25% unemployment; and worst of all, it took a decade to recover.

According to Keynesian economic models, the market goes up and down because the market reacts according to emotions. In other words, it is irrational. After the crash of 2008, a study at University of Chicago determined that the economy is rational. However, according to Lerner of Harvard University, the market is absolutely affected by human emotions. Thus the market can be, and is, irrational. According to her, many people in the market behave differently when they are happy as opposed to when they are sad in any given circumstance. Robert Shiller of Credit Suisse says that although we communicate with words, the sharing of feelings is the main purpose of our communication. Empathy that is communicated from one human being to another via words is exactly what drives our behavior, and thus our economy.

Then, somewhere in the program, there was the assertion that if and when a market is efficient, it really does not need any regulations. This assertion is now of monumental importance. In this digital economy, any waste, and market deception will become obvious in minutes, hours, or days as opposed to months or even years. So, as the Six Million Dollar Man said, "We have the technology. Let's use it."

If we use proper management processes and/practices, such as the HP Way, the company will run so efficiently, with a high level of mutual trust and loyalty, that none of these layoffs, strikes, and downsizings will be needed. Do not be surprised that instead of whatever awful unemployment we now have; we can have a 107.8% employment! That's the subject of one of my future books.

If our corporations and small businesses were more careful about managing their strategic and tactical planning and operations, these massive and frequent layoffs are not needed. Remember that HP did not lay off *even one* employee during the first fifty years of its existence.

Layoffs kill hope, and they kill the fundamental American strength of innovation. There has to be enough CEO and Board of Directors accountability to prevent these kinds of things. One of the most famous economists said that the recent recession seems to have killed American hope. If this is the case, according to him, America is in much bigger trouble than just a bad economy.

When $60 billion of hard-earned wealth disappears in the stock market in a few weeks or months, there is something drastically wrong.

As for me, I will light a candle – or even light a torch, like the one in the hand of the Statue of Liberty – rather than have this doom and gloom that result from cursing the darkness. I hope that your sentiments are similar to mine.

As a result of our work serving the White House on the job creation committee, I have included these plans of action for America as well as for you and me. We want America to become that respected and honored global ultra power, and we want ourselves to be continue to work during these turbulent years.

To those who are now propagating this doom-mongering self-fulfilling hopelessness, let me warn them that they are wrong.

We are moving from an era of "Debt and Destruction" thinking to a new era of "Rewards and Digital Humanity". In this new era, our technology will drive a high demand on optimal usage of human intellectual property as the primary driver of our future global success. While this is true for organizations, this is even more evident and true for individuals as well.

We as individuals need to invest in ourselves by gaining education on a life-long basis and update our education in an ongoing basis. We need to plan and indeed be the CEO of our own career and life. Since our best job security is ourselves and the on demand, marketable, and certifiable skill set that we have. In America, we can do and be anything that we want to.

Also, considering the fact that small businesses are the backbone of the American business and that small businesses are one of the biggest job engines, it might be that our best interest as individuals can be served by having our own small business or working for a small business. As you can see on the cover of my book, the future will belong to one or two person companies running from a kitchen with a smart phone or laptop while serving an important business need.

With a proper plan of action and its execution, we will succeed. After all, according to former Secretary of State, the Honorable George Shultz, "Bruce, this is America! We can say and do anything we want!"

Let's follow the plan of action for our country and ourselves that is presented in Appendix A and B.

Please Contact: bruce@razban.com

CHAPTER 19
Future can be as Bright and Profitable as you want

During the thirty years that I have volunteered to help those who were unemployed, I have discovered a common "situational depression, wet blanket, and what is the use?" attitude and approach.

Again, please realize that I am not a psychologist. I am a management consultant and executive coach. So, what I'm writing here has to be taken within that context.

The clinical depression is simple to define. A person is so sad and disappointed that she cannot do the normal daily chores. However, there are other depressions that happen when something goes wrong. A person who gets unexpectedly fired will be sad and not able to do the normal activities expected of him. If this condition goes away after a while, then the depression is lifted. If it persists more than a few days, one needs to see a therapist and/or a psychiatrist.

Typically those who are affected with this will need to get immediate professional help. However, just the existence of situational depression deters any action needed to overcome the condition in the first place.

In most management cases, using the Six Sigma process, we can quickly find the root cause of a potential project failure and act on it as the primary problem.

A job, in some cases any job, can go a long way in a speedy recovery from situational depression. This does not negate the need for seeking and getting professional help.

A secondary side-effect of this is when people get so preoccupied with the standard fixation resulting from depression they forget that some income can go a long way in alleviating the situation. Depression is nothing to be ashamed of. It is a biological imbalance that can be treated by proper medication.

My kid brother, on one occasion, gave me a bundle of $20 bills. After putting a full tank of gas in my car, I rushed to my favorite restaurant and treated myself to my most favorite dish that costs $19.95. Then a badly needed haircut, a carwash, and still having another $40 left over. This made my mood a lot better.

So, what we need here is to be aware of this situational depression and get treatment. However, we still need to do our

117

planning and working on a brighter future.

Remember that exercise about job inventory, your job description for your ideal job, and then deciding what you really want to do? All that will help, and help immensely. I know that when I keep busy on some interesting project, I tend to forget my sorrows.

There was a joke that used to say that we need to soar like an eagle even if we are surrounded by turkeys. Wet blankets are people who will discourage us from doing anything. This is usually done in best of the intensions, yet it is damaging.

I typically listen to what they say. Then, I carefully analyze it. In some cases, one of these wet blankets, out of jealousy, was trying to convince me not to do what he was doing.

This is the time to dust off doom and gloom, since in my opinion these are un-American luxuries, along with hate and discrimination, that we cannot afford, especially now. This is the time when we need to become the America that the world expects us to be, to lead, empower, and free them. As the Six Million Dollar Man TV series used to say, "We have the technology! In addition to that, we have the innovative courage to do what it takes to save us and the world."

Get your incorporation done, put together your business plan, and each day act on all the action items that you can within your human-best abilities. Call Legal Zoom or another such firm to get started on your own Incorporation Libration. Once started, you will agree with me that this is much easier than you might have thought!

Now we get to the "What's the Use?" part. Let me tell you that not only it is good for your future to be solvent; it's also great for our country as well as the entire globe!

The recent events including the double-digit unemployment, negative and pessimistic economic picture, epidemic of hopelessness, and toxic work place that tends to be causing a great deal of job related unhappiness have all horrified all of us. As such, we must be proactive in finding a job and/or starting our own business.

My 32 years of working in Silicon Valley tells me the best time to start a new company is during economic down times like this.

I'm optimistic that America will do what America is expected to do, and be the leader of the free world and the entire globe. Just like John F. Kennedy put a man on the moon, we need to make sure that the global financial situation is better than what we see now.

America has the material and human resources to be the globes only ultra-power, while letting many others, including China and India, become superpowers.

This is done by actively pursuing your life and work dreams. Make sure that you never give up 20 minutes before the miracle.

Thus, with all this Global Financial Crisis, you will be a CEO of your life and career, if you plan and then execute on that.

Please Contact: bruce@razban.com

CHAPTER 20
Future of Work and Jobs in the Globe and You

Some years ago, a tiny start-up in Sunnyvale, in the heart of the Silicon Valley, started an excellent idea. The idea was simple. Suppose you were an employer and wanted some software project to get done. Let us say that you had the project definition and requirements done. Then you'd put that project on eLance.com and ask for people who felt confident to bid.

Eventually, after reviewing all the bids, you would then hire someone and sign a contract. The idea is as powerful as it is simple. Let's say that you want to go from point A to point B. You can either decide to buy a car, or rent a car. The eLance idea is similar to renting an expertise rather than hiring that expertise and being stuck with management and a lot of related overhead for it.

On the eLance website, there were hundreds of people from all around the globe who were advertising what their skill-set, expertise, and rates were. At first there were only Americans who charged a fee per hour that was not that much lower than the market rate. Some years later the competition got a lot worse. There were people from Eastern Europe, the Middle East, or other places saying they had the needed expertise and would do the job for a fraction of what work would pay in Silicon Valley.

It's my firm belief that soon, people develop one or more marketable and certifiable expertise and work on several projects for several companies each day. I went into great detail about this in *Layoffs and Hope*.

Just to make the point clear, let's say that you've worked as a full-time employee for an accounting firm for a long time. Let's say that you've become an expert in all aspects of accounts payable. Then, in a process similar to eLance, you advertise your expertise and start getting bids on different projects. Most likely, you will be working out of a home office.

So, on a daily basis, you might be working two hours for an Australian company, four hours for a Napa Valley winery, and the rest of the day you will work for a Chicago merchandising company. In other words, this will be a production line process where you sell your bottled expertise!

The rest of this book is devoted to helping you succeed in this turbulent workplace. I do my best to use the thirty years of experience that I've had to help you plan and then execute on creating a job for you that puts you in charge, motivates you to succeed, and helps you to be happy in this difficult work place.

Ever since I saw my best friend and colleague disappear by a simple layoff edict, I decided that I would do my best so nobody should go through that again.

The decision that day is finally taking shape and becoming zestfully alive in these pages!

Going back to the HP school of management, I wonder,

- What if we re-invented our declining businesses by using the best management practices from Original Joe's or the HP of the good old days, before all the scandals and less than superior management?

- What if we realized that China has all the inexpensive manufacturing power that it needs, and we were happy to buy the American apple pie pan from them, even with the "Made in China" stamp on it. We're still preserving our Johnny Appleseed tradition and keeping American jobs. In this totally interconnected and interdependent global village economy, job loss in China or India does not necessarily translate into job gain in the US or the other way around. We must co-operate to create a real job win-win for all.

- What if we did what we do best, which excludes cheap manufacturing but is inventiveness and entrepreneurship?

- What if we encouraged, admired, and even worshiped, business champions like Warren Buffet, Fredrick Smith, and Sir Branson? In a way, instead of having military generals and commanders, or equal to them, we now have economy generals and business leaders and commanders.

- What if the American private sector generated ten or twenty Twitters, eBays, and more important, Googles? We can do this. This is our cup of tea. This kind of thing runs in American blood and DNA.
- Did you know that eBay was started by Pierre Omidyar trying to sell Pez dispensers online? He wrote the code himself. This is the proof of American ingenuity in finding a market need and American knowhow to build that better mouse trap, along with entrepreneurship. We can do wonders, and can get us out of this Global Financial Crisis.
- Pierre has reinvented eBay and Twitter, thus showing that we can clone and reinvent American prowess in innovation and value-added marketing.
- Google was dream of two Israeli immigrants, Larry Page and Sergey Brin, trying to put all the information in this world in a suitcase.
- Did you know that Professor David Cheriton of Stanford University was Larry and Sergey's professor, who empowered them and helped them start the company that now is Google by giving them their first Venture Capital check?
- Did you know that even Professor Cheriton, in an interview with BBC, was getting to be resigned to how bad the American economy can become? However, I tend to disagree with him.
- I'm convinced that as Americans we will make poor penny-pinchers and austerity-confined lives. As Americans, we can dream, and dream big! If we were to not buy houses until we had the money, the housing industry would go to hell! If we did not put wisely managed and fortified money in circulation, our banking system will collapse. If we did not consume, our economy would self-destruct. Money is only important and effective when it circulates, and not when it is printed or saved!
- With all due respect to the government, we need to

fortify their efforts in job creation in the private sector.

- What if we stopped the idea of hiring cheap labor and working them to death; charging the consumer as much as we can; take the money and run, but instead treated our employees and customers as if they were our close relatives?
- What if Wall Street did pay attention to human capital, long term, and seriously looked beyond management gimmicks and speculations?
- What good did any of these multi-billion dollar corporate buying, acquisitions, and mergers do for the long-term and overall well-being of our economy and humanity?
- Is it not time for us to create prosperity for ourselves and the world by proactive, profitable, philanthropy instead of blind money-mongering and ambition that does not care if our actions are devastating to all in the long term?
- What if it was the lack of good American management that got us into this Global Financial Crisis, dragging the rest of the world into it too?
- To those who confuse management with control and empty regulations, try to run an airport without management, and good management. You'd have a zoo on your hands. We've reached a point that we need global management to prevent the next Global Financial Crisis. Just like the days when United Nations was started in San Francisco, we need a new, reinvented, impartial, and effective United Nations, and even IMF, just like the way they were envisioned when they were founded in San Francisco some fifty or so years ago.
- Can you imagine what could have happened with Hurricane Irene if we had not managed it?
- Was it not management that was the name of the game in preventing catastrophe when Irene hit?

- Is it not tiny small business cottage industries that are easy to create that can create jobs?
- What if knee-jerk reaction massive and frequent layoffs can easily and more profitably replaced by better management of our precious material and human intellectual capital?
- With the right core values, superb customer value-added products and services, we can still beat any global competition.
- It was these same core values and inventiveness and entrepreneurship that empowered Mr. Hewlett and Mr. Packard to turn an ordinary Palo Alto garage into a world-class company that hired hundreds of thousands of people.

You might be thinking that these things take a lot of hard work. You might be right. However, trust me that it is by far more difficult to be unemployed than do what it takes to find and keep a good job or be the founder of the next HP or Google, or Facebook. The pain and suffering that unemployment or underemployment causes is by far more that what it takes to be working. In fact the joy of working for yourself as the CEO of your company by far exceeds any amount of work needed to be an entrepreneur and create your own company.

Make a habit of calling your friends who are doing what you like to do and buy them lunch and ask them how you can do what they did. Suppose you want to open a flower shop. Ask around among your friends and find who has a flower shop. Or just go to different shops and ask.

Then one step at a time you will make progress towards your goal. Remember that a Chinese proverb says a journey of million miles starts with a single step.

Take that step today!

Please Contact: bruce@razban.com

CHAPTER 21
Incorporation Libration

Would it not be nice if we all enjoyed a great deal of job security and worked for just a single employer who was solid? Would it not be nice if that employer, in alliance with us, helped us constantly enhance and improve our skill set? Remember, a higher index of intellectual capitalism creates higher income for a company. Would it not be nice if we did not have to constantly be worried about layoffs or waste our time and energy in workplace politics? Would it not be nice if we had mutual trust and loyalty between employees and management, and company and customers?

That would be extremely nice! Unfortunately, in many cases that luxury is not there anymore. My career, and that of many of my colleagues, is proof that many of us have had to keep jumping around so as not to be hit by massive and frequent layoffs. I, for one, would have wanted to work, and work as hard as possible and be as dedicated as possible until retirement for Zilog, Inc., HP, TeleStream, EXP.com, Egghead.com which is now part of the Amazon.com, Kaiser Permanente, PayPal, eBay, Cisco, National Semiconductor Corporation, or any of the others that I worked for.

My longest employer was National Semiconductor Corporation (NSC)! I worked there for almost nine years. As part of my job, I got to travel all around the world, and I worked for some outstanding executives, such as Giora Yaron. Giora was an Israeli who was in charge of NSC in Tel Aviv. He was a no-nonsense executive who delivered quality products, who NSC could rely on.

However, the executive who really shaped my career, and shaped it for the better, was Dr. Gil Amelio. He was Charlie Spork's replacement. Charlie Spork was the founder, and later on the CEO, of NSC, and he handpicked Dr. Gil Amelio as his successor.

Dr. Gil Amelio inherited a company that was having frequent layoffs, and was struggling to have enough money for the next paychecks to be paid. He decided that he had to transform the culture and the spirit of the company by teaching managers how to manage. With intense help from Emory University, he personally conducted a series of management training sessions called

"Leading Change." His strategic and tactical leading change efforts took hold, and NSC became a solid and respectable company again. You, too, can transform your career by being your own leading change leader CEO! Otherwise, you might end up being disappointed, unemployed, or underemployed, or unhappily employed for some time to come, just as I did.

As much as I liked working for NSC, there came the time to say goodbye!

A big layoff was in the works, and in spite all the efforts by the VP, there was no way that they could keep me and several others who had been dedicated workers and outstanding employees. In my case, I was one the few who'd gotten a patent grant, and the company was really proud of that.

Soon, it became obvious to me that I wouldn't get a permanent job as a regular employee elsewhere, and I had to learn to become a full-time consultant. My repeated resume sending was getting nowhere, and even when I went to interviews, the hiring managers always found some reason or the other to not hire me. In one case, Mr. Nitin rejected me for three different jobs at three different companies. Fact remains that I was more than qualified for all three jobs!

Also, age was a major parameter. In one of my published management articles regarding plain age discrimination, I described in vivid detail how ugly this was. The article is called *Ageism Rageism*.

"Bruce you cannot do this to your family! You're putting them at risk. Go get a job, any job! Bruce you need health insurance. How will you get that?" These were severe objections that I heard from many colleagues and friends. So each day, I would meekly send resumes into that cyber black hole that is the burial place of resumes. I did lots of networking, and the entire job finding stuff that by now I had become a champion at.

One day I found the courage and decided to call LegalZoom and ask them how much it would cost to incorporate. The price was far lower than I'd anticipated. Thus, in a short while, Razban Internet International, Incorporated was born. I got all the forms and stamps that were needed to conduct as an official Incorporation and with the proper image, and I was in business.

Since my patent while I was working at NSC, and in conjunction with HP, had created a $5 million product line for HP and saved NSC another $10 million in testing, I was determined to get patents pending for my later inventions. My next patent was a revolutionary one in making Object Oriented computation a lot easier. Soon, I got help from many well-wishers and Don, who is a Stanford University Ph.D. who used to work for me at Zilog, and then we worked together at NSC. Don's advisor is now president of Stanford University. Using every bit of what I had learned from the Stanford seminar, "How to Start a Successful Startup," I worked day and night. I'm sure that you want the next paragraph to say, "And, I became a multimillionaire!"

Unfortunately, I did not! The Stanford course was right. However, it was the 2008 stock market crash and a drop of more than 400 points in the Dow Jones Index and the Bank of America deciding not to issue any new loans that stopped my progress dead at its tracks before I could really get started.

I decided that I'd look at the glass as 10% full instead of the part that was 90% empty. With that inspiring attitude, I empowered myself to work as hard as I could without getting discouraged, or even tired.

I had to swallow my pride and jettison what was left of my dignity, and do the "beg, borrow, but not steal," thing. As the foreclosure got worse and worse, I decided to use the only winning card I had. That winning card was to publish three books that were on Amazon.com, Barnes and Noble, and several independent bookstores, such as Kepler's in Menlo Park.

Since I was experienced in working with venture capitalists, I experienced firsthand what patent violation meant when part of my patent was copied and used in India, and I had no legal possibility of claiming or recovering any of it.

"Bruce let's face it! The fact that they are using it is proof that it was a good one. You still have the other parts of that!" was a best friend and colleague's caring and soothing words to get me out of my anger and depression. Now that my company was incorporated, with that "Inc." at the end, meant that people were taking me more and more seriously.

Then there was the issue of insurance. As an independent consultant, one has to purchase insurance to protect companies from suing. This, too, was extremely easy. I purchased about $1 million dollars' worth of insurance by paying only $30 per month.

I did some heavy soul-searching, and found out that my most marketable skill-set is that of management. Also, soon I realized that the most marketable part of my skill-set was program and project management. I had seen many HPers and IBMers do the same.

As you can see, it is not that difficult to follow the same step-by step-process and really become CEO or President of your company and life in a legal and down-to-earth way.

To look even more official, go to the FedEx nearest your house or work and get business cards printed.

Right after this, I found the job search a lot more palatable. I send one resume for some promising and sexy job, and send another one for finding a client who would hire consultants. Consultants are hired either under a W2 arrangement, which is the traditional way, or 1095 or 1099 which is what we can do now, since you have incorporated. Generally, there is a great tax advantage in 1095 or 1099. However, W2 is the more common way, and you need not worry about payroll taxes and quarterly tax payments.

Soon, as the economy got better, I was able to find a client who paid excellent wages. While I worked there, I learned new things each and every day.

This is then the way I've earned a living since 1996.

The interesting thing is that by "incorporation libration," which is the title of this chapter, I was able to literally liberate myself from the chains that pay check dependence had put on my neck. I could work when I wanted, and generally I could choose the contracts that made sense for me.

My tax accountant of many years has decided to put a higher importance on family than just work. His wife who is also his business partner works with him in a three room office. In another room his two younger daughters are playing with artwork and making picture frames. During my meeting with my outstanding tax accountant, his five year old daughter knocked at the door and asked for dad to give her some Scotch tape. Dad gave her the Scotch tape and then picked her up to give her a big hug and a kiss.

This is an excellent example of Incorporation Libration! Dad and mom take care of their kids during the time that they are not in school while they also do their daily work. As a senior management and technology consultant, I had realized that the work done by this couple or better yet, this family has been outstanding and superb.

Remember that executive who told me in San Jose

Executive Jet Port that his biggest regret in life is that he did not spend enough time with his kids as they were growing up. He was blaming himself for being much too busy trying to make money to make his family happy.

No such thing will be here.

Mom and dad are there all the time while doing their work too. Let us do some calculations on this:

- Assuming that a person graduates at the age of 22 and works until he or she is 66, then they have spent as much as 88,704 hours at work!

- Of these 88,704 hours perhaps a less than half percent (.5%) might be spent on taking care of the kids during an 8 hour work day.

- I had seen the same calming effect in several of my colleagues when they had finally decided to become CEO of their own career and life and operate out of a kitchen table or small office. My tax accountant in particular seemed to try to tell me, "Bruce put it in perspective. Your health and family is by far worth more than millions of dollars!"

- In early 1980s, I saw exactly the same in a friend who decided to make a Starbucks-like coffee shop where the entire family will be together for several hours during the day. He did this many decades before Starbucks and others became a gathering place for people to be together. There is a great deal of value in being there and on being together. This friend and colleague was a senior software architect with a Masters Degree from a world-famous university

- Another colleague decided to work in airport security just to get away from the daily rat race of corporate world and then have a three day weekend each and every week to spend with his loved ones.

- In addition being in Silicon Valley for as many years as I have been, I must say that I admire and respect Steve Jobs as a marketing genius. Furthermore, I do know that a lot of people did not approve of his management style. However, one thing that is critically important to note is that each and every night he would go home for dinner. The entire family would get together and try to carry on an interesting discussion around that non-descript kitchen table that they had for many, many years.

- I also never forget my friend and colleague who work for

Caltrans which is a government office for California Highways. The last time I saw him, he was proudly showing off his tie that his daughter had given him for his birthday. Then he would tell me, "Bruce my family is everything to me. I cannot wait to become a grandfather. I live just for my kids and wife." He had been an outstanding employee for several years and with several recommendations to show for it. Thus, the point is not that we need to do a skimpy job at work or spoil our loved ones and family at the expense of an honest day's job. The point is that we can do both and being anchored in a healthy family life; we can accomplish more at work so it becomes a win-win situation.

- Another example is that of a famous consultant who was in high demand for his extremely valuable skills in fixing certain navigation systems in aircraft careers and cruise ships. He would be the Guru that they would go to fix some of the most complicated systems. He told me that since career forced him to go to many different parts of the world, he made a point of always taking an hour off each they to spend with his family no matter where he was on any sea. He always called, and wrote letters during that time that he was away on business trips as if he was with his family.

Unfortunately, I am also seeing a bad side of the so called social networking these days too. I see young couples where they are both busy sending and receiving text or email messages that they do not have time for each other.

I see so many colleagues that are trained super and aggressive achievers who are programmed to get it all and get it all at any price.

My regret is that some day they too would realize their mistake just like that executive who told me he wished he had lived more and spent more time with his loved ones.

Blind ambition and subhuman greed has destroyed so many people and lives that make me very sad. If a man or woman is destructively fixated on success and success at any price, they sooner or later realize a black hole of emptiness in their lives that no amount of money can buy or fix. In contrast, those who decide to have job and life satisfaction and be with their loved ones, they find a happiness that no amount of money can buy when they say no to blind ambition and greed!

Please Contact: bruce@razban.com

CHAPTER 22
Digital Humanity and Intellectual Materialism

The digital economy will affect all aspects of our lives. Social networking and iPods and tablets will drastically change the way we live. President Eisenhower's "Military Industrial Complex" will be replaced by Digital Humanity and Intellectual Capitalism which is a positive approach.

You might recall the story I told you about profit-sharing checks at Plantronics. This was a story of all of us going out of our way to find a better solution for a company based on mutual trust and loyalty.

In an industry conference some time later, I heard an executive from another company boasting about his company having so many orders, and that it can produce one headset in such-and-such time. I knew that Plantronics numbers were not that high, but I was amazed to hear the response from one of our Plantronics executives. She told him, "While I respect your numbers, let me tell you that our team is the best. Several members just got higher degrees; we published several articles in a prestigious magazine; and we have almost zero turnover rate. Also, one more thing, our employees offered to work without pay to save $3,000 for the company. We paid all the educational expenses for our night shift janitor to become an excellent expert in injection molding plastic that was vital to Plantronics products. This mutual trust and loyalty has paid off handsomely! We're really proud of him and proud of ourselves for having done the right thing for employees and customers. Doing the honorable right thing is good and profitable management." That Plantronics executive knew what she was talking about. She had learned that human intellectual capital manifested itself in better work processes, and knowledge in company's core competence is more important than just plain material-based Capitalism.

In 1981, I was managing an engineering team that developed the Z-Scan80. We worked on the hardware and software, and then integrated them. As far as we were concerned, we were developing a tool for computer designers to use. For example, a hammer is a tool. We had a narrow and intense focus on only technical things.

Fast forward some thirty or forty years. The same narrow-mindedness of producing a purely technical solution for a technical problem remains.

In other words, we have not learned how to look at the human aspect of what our tools are about. Same as 1982, I'm willing to bet that when Twitter was being designed, there were no thoughts of maybe it does a good thing for human beings and creates an opportunity for people to fight back guns and bullets by digital information. Internet-speed information, available instantly and everywhere, has empowered the opposition groups to successfully get rid of their dictators.

Maybe when the design requirements were written for FaceBook, there were no psychological studies dealing with the isolation and depression that this product makes, in addition to all other great things about it.

Next time you go to a restaurant, or wait for a bus or a train, please observe how the so-called social networks have created antisocial behavior. You will see a couple sitting facing each other in a restaurant while they are both deeply immersed in their iPod, Blackberry, iPhone, or other tool, rather than having a warm conversation face to face with another human being. Worse yet, I have several times been almost hit by somebody trying to text and walk at the same time, who bumps into me. A few weeks ago, I noticed an angry man shaking his finger at me and telling me that I was stupid as he was approaching me. As he got closer, I realized that he was not talking to me. He was talking to his jawbone cell phone earpiece that was plugged into his ear. However, it did indeed look like he was looking into my eyes and telling me that I was stupid.

Digital humanity will change everything, including our government, advertising, and daily activity. Imagine that a day-to-day tally of promises against actual performance for politicians can be on public notice in seconds. More importantly, imagine that an insurance company's advertising has a real-time indicator of the percentage of happy customers shown right on the screen. Therefore, the good old truth in advertising has now become rule-based data tabulations that our information technology systems can do in a blink of the eye.

Just as Professor Dietmeyer of the University of Wisconsin said, in the digital era, everything can be either true or false. For example, either employees are happy or they are not. Either the latest round of layoffs killed thirty percent of mutual trust and loyalty or it did not. Remember it is either true or false as they are represented in a computer in a series of 1s and 0s.

Sooner or later, our management training and day to day activity will force us to take human and intellectual materialism and Capitalism in full attention the same way that we care for and handle material capitalism.

This will force us to take into account the human impact of every little part of the requirement statement or design rules such as job creation or destruction should be considered from the beginning. This forces us to convert human misery into human prosperity as we go about running of our daily business.

I admire my Apple iPhone3 as it is a lot more understanding of human needs and desires than many other devices in the market. The old human factors analysis was done well in this product. Therefore, let us think how much things could be better if the human cost of American unemployment could have been considered in the financial equations when out sourcing was being considered. This is such a straight forward calculation that many of my MBA students at Keller Graduate School of Management can do easily.

Perhaps then some of these super smart gadgets of the future will be not only be location aware, but also human mental and physical health aware. We can do this with the technology that we have available today.

One thing that the digital economy has done is that it has eliminated all guessing, politics, and downright lies by using the digital cash register honesty of company cultures, processes, and daily activities.

In turn, all those executives who had obtained an MBA from the Gadhafy School of management will be in trouble with the digital era. Those 1s and 0s will make it impossible for scare tactics and customer dissatisfaction to continue for any long period of time without bankrupting the company.

Please Contact: bruce@razban.com

CHAPTER 23
In the End, it is You, Your Life, Your Career, and Your Dreams

You do deserve a reward for reading this far in this book. I hope that this book has empowered and inspired you to thrive in your life, career, and work. I hope that this book has energized you to not give up minutes before the miracle and having the Israeli type of chutzpa to challenge seemingly impossible hurdles to win against all odds as this is the American mentality and approach to life as well. This is the American knowhow, the American spirit of being the world and now the interconnected global leader. This is the American Spirit that the Nazi, the 911, and the infamous Pearl Harbor devastating attacks could not defeat. I you have decided to be that CEO of your life and career that is formulated here to succeed in the turbulent work life that faces us as the Global Financial Crisis unfolds. I hope that you have the Japanese style courage, discipline, and success culture to overcome the aftermath of Hiroshima type setback before and now the Tsunami and floods.

You might be working for the government, a major corporation, a start up or you might be unemployed, under-employed, or unhappily employed. However, you all have the opportunity to change odds that are against you to odds that are in your favor and give meaning, excitement, and success to your career and life by following the simple steps formulated here to actually build your own triple-decker career bus in a journey to success based on your main, standby, and desperation jobs and career plans and following your dream until success.

Recently, on their occasion of their fiftieth anniversary, the Rolling Stones divulged their secret to success as:
- Do not work for anybody else,
- Do not work for money,
- Do what makes you happy.

I take their advice to heart as they are the experts in making their career a huge success and them, as the singers of the song, "I can get no satisfaction" must know the secrets of satisfaction!

Here are the simple steps needed to succeed:

1. Review and focus on your own answers regarding what you will do if you had won millions of dollars and never had to work again another day in your life.
2. Review your own answers regarding what you will do as a hobby, or on a vacation.
3. The above two help clarify what will be meaningful to you as the CEO in charge of your life and career.
4. Being your own boss and in charge, write down your own "Ideal Job Description" to your heart's satisfaction.
5. Review the above with people you respect and those who seem to be successful in their lives and careers, friends, and family. Ask them to be positive and supportive as well as realistic.
6. Revise and edit the above as many times as you like.
7. Write down and classify above in three different categories of:
   a. Primary career,
   b. Stand-by career,
   c. Desperation job(s)
8. Prepare a one minute "Elevator Pitch" for each in writing. This means that if you had one minute in an elevator with a total stranger in your field of expertise how you can describe the exact type of job that you want. We are talking about your dream career.
9. Now, close your eyes and imagine that you have gotten that ideal job. We have a saying that says, "Fake it Until You Make it!" So, in a nice and quiet place, pretend you have the job. Conduct a make believe interview of yourself with yourself about the job success and life happiness.
10. Back to step 9, try to realistically talk about the life satisfaction that the job satisfaction regarding your doing the ideal job will bring for you. Watch out for jobs that are extremely satisfying but jobs that destroy your life and family life. Remember that we are looking for a win-win situation.
11. Write major steps on how to get that ideal work and life. Then add details to that so you have a monthly, weekly, and even daily plan of action items to do to get or keep this ideal situation.
12. Each day pick up your phone and call friends, family, old colleagues, and acquaintances. Do not ask for a job but get them interested in helping you find a job. Remember that you looking for somebody who might know somebody who might

know somebody else that might know about a job. After each call write down a quick summary about what they told you and more importantly always end these networking calls with either let us get together for lunch or coffee, or please permit me to call you back later on.

13. Each day "Google" your way to success by doing two things on Google:
    a. Look for jobs and directly apply to them,
    b. Learn about the subject matters that are important to your career, and companies in your field and check their job openings.
    c. Generally by using your city name, state, and job title as search words in Google you will be impressed with how many jobs are available in your area of search.
    d. Remember that a lot of job descriptions are inflated. Apply for each job that you have about 50% of the requirements with a vanilla type resume, and a custom-made resume for those that you more than 75% qualified.
    e. Make sure to also include working as an intern or a volunteer for nonprofit and charity companies. This will give you the experience that you might not have had as well as opens the door to other jobs.

14. In parallel with this, think about the Incorporation Liberation. Call Legal Zoom or other similar services to get your incorporation done.

15. Now that you are delightfully pursuing the dream of being your own CEO as well as getting a job as a regular employee or consultant, there is a feeling of empowerment that will bring you a great deal of satisfaction, self-respect, and satisfaction along with a feeling of being productive. After all success means living happily and doing what is humanly possible for one day at a time and not more and no less.

16. Each day make sure that you spend time on learning something new in your career. For this youtube.com might very well be the best. It almost feels like you are watching a movie, but they now have fantastic movie clips on anything that can be educational, entertaining, or even strange.

17. Find and learn from other people who are doing the same thing in your field. Many of the people including you that will

be happy to help others by being their mentor, teacher, guru, or advisor.

18. Whether you have a full time job or not, try on your incorporation side to find your first customer.
19. Close that first sales and learn as much as possible from it.
20. Seek other sales, contracts, and/or work.

Remember that we as Americans have two very important sayings:

- The price of freedom is constant vigil. This means that we constantly, even when we are successfully and gainfully working for a company or our own incorporated company must look for that next job, career, customer, educational chance to increase our work and life related skill set, and

- Freedom is not free. We might have to invest in our freedom to continue to be free.

I hope that this book has empowered and inspired you to thrive in finding and keeping an excellent job in these turbulent times.

You can most definitely be the CEO of your career and life that you are intended to be. At the end it is worth a lot of happiness.

Please Contact: <u>bruce@razban.com</u>

APPENDIX A
Executive Summary

Since, you are now empowered to be the CEO of your life and career, let me give you a taste of an executive summaries. An executive summary is of course a summary. However, it is extremely precise and packed with logical, related, and important facts and figures. Better executive summaries usually contain actionable conclusions with sufficient analysis and justification with clear set of consequences and pros and cons!

Evidenced by "Occupy Wall Street" demonstrations all around the world that started in Columbus Day of 2011 as predicted or suggested by this book, America is in cross hairs of Iraq, Afghanistan, and economics crisis/wars!

Chronic high unemployment, hints of potential return of recession, and hopelessness has bitterly divided America and is beginning to break European Unity's Euro Zone! For the first time in a century next generation Americans will have lower standard of living than their fathers and mothers had.

At the time of this writing, the uprising in London, which unfortunately was not peaceful, is put down – perhaps for some time. However, the flames can be rekindled as a result of Occupied Wall Street. In Palo Alto, Bank of America was the dominant focus of the protests.

Soon, other business institutions will also become the first focus of protests.

A moment of depressing and agonizing will soon arrive where no matter what the focus is, we must think teamwork and win-win solutions. As we learned in Vietnam War, breaking windows is the easy part; building and creating social change for the better is the difficult part.

After all the dust is settled and talk show hosts and so called talking heads on TV are done "talking without saying anything!" then massive collaboration will start.

The old American material-based capitalism is dead! It has been dead since its death was announced in a Kevin Covey writing.

A new and improved reinvented American capitalism took effect that bloody day in 2008 that Wall Street dropped 400 points in one single day!

My first book, Layoffs and Hope, declared that the new

capitalism had to take into account two important things and integrate them in the new modern Global American Reinvented Capitalism. These two things were intellectual capital and Internet.

Advent of social networking and immense impact of Internet created Arab Spring. The same two things have now created Occupied Wall Street.

Economists at Harvard and Stanford University among many other places are studying and for that matter have been recommending for some time for businesses to reduce and even detangle themselves from Wall Street by becoming masters of their own destiny. This movement is exactly what this book is also recommending by saying that we need to become CEOs of our lives and our careers.

An effective and easy way to understand step-by-step solution tells us how we can get and keep a job as the CEO of our own life and career to cope and even thrive in these turbulent economic times!

APPENDIX B:
Mr. Razban's Report to the White House Job Creation
Committee as a Silicon Valley Community Leader

In research done by Stanford University, it was found that the root cause for many addictions is a false assumption. For example, an alcoholic might be totally convinced that he/she can stop drinking any time. Another important research study, also from Stanford University, finds that the best way to deal with anger is forgiveness. However, in order to forgive, one first has to deal with the "narrative," which is typically an untrue or exaggerated story, similar to the false assumptions that addicts have invented. Unfortunately, this narrative, that has festered and evolved for many years, is so true in the addict's mind that it can totally eclipse reality and frustrate any attempts by the victim to let go of the fixation, and that would prevent any action to cope, recover, or even thrive.

Silicon Valley CA is a hotbed of the most powerful high-tech companies, like Google, HP, Intel, etc. Life is much faster here than anywhere else in terms of companies, from starting up to total devastation. Therefore, Silicon Valley can serve as an excellent laboratory to observe economic and business phenomena.

As a Senior Management and Technology Consultant with 32 years experience, I have carefully studied the entire life cycle of jobs and ecosystems from creation to layoffs and firings. In addition, during the eight years it took for me to write *Layoffs & Hope*, I have made several conclusions that can be extremely helpful in President Obama's job creation program. In the 1980s, I suffered from unemployment for many months. Then there was the dot-com crash that resulted in nine months of joblessness and hopelessness. Each of these downturns, and my intensive volunteer work helping unemployed, underemployed and unhappily employed, were proof-positive about the correctness of my conclusions.

The narrative that the present financial crisis was solely created by banks giving easy loans is a dangerously faulty assumption that will prevent our attempts to deal effectively with this crisis and create jobs. The root cause of this faulty assumption is that the economy and business are considered the same way as the weather. The same way that we believe that weather is out of our control, we have been brainwashed to think that the economy, like the weather, is unmanageable. The free market is so poorly handled that it resembles a free-fall market. The free market cannot stay free without due diligence exercised in any merger or acquisition.

Fact 1: For the free market to operate and be successful, we must have self-imposed governance that is totally transparent and effective. For example, SOX needs to be expanded. We must have a consumer rights watchdog as powerful as the Underwriters Laboratory (UL) that prevents dangerous electrical products from being marketed. For example, any aircraft from any part of the world is free to fly to any other part of the world. Such freedom can only be guaranteed via an air traffic control system, and global practical, actionable, protocols and conventions.

Fact 2: The Internet has been by far a more powerful revolution than the industrial revolution. Unfortunately, our financial, trade, educational, and economic systems have failed to keep pace and harness the power.

Fact 3: The Internet revolution has created two massive game-changers:

a) Information available instantly anywhere, a phenomenon that was instrumental in coordinating and enabling millions of people in many countries to successfully accomplish the Arab Spring, and

b) Human and Intellectual Capital becoming just as, if not more, important than the traditional "Things Capital." American capitalism that is based on the freedom, democracy, and human rights needs to re-invent itself and create amendments to cope, recover, and even thrive from this. Kevin Covey has been saying this for two years, now. Proof of this pudding is India. Just a few years ago, before the Java technology, India was not a rich country. Now India is the center of IT excellence. This was mainly done with human intellectual capitalism.

Fact 3: Even at an "ideal" 4% unemployment, there is a $2.4 Trillion prosperity producing productivity loss that can be saved by doing things differently.

Fact 4: We need business, government, and consumers;

that is, all three, to do teamwork to create a win-win solution to this financial crisis.

Fact 5: CEOs and Boards of Directors, instead of isolating themselves and being out of touch with market and consumer realities, and benefiting from sky-high salaries, are resented immensely. The example of the future successful CEO is that of Sir Richard Branson, of Virgin Group. He is a rock star, evangelist, and superb communicator, who empowers his employees to generate the highest level of mutual trust and loyalty to produce high productivity and success.

Consumer resentment goes beyond selectivity at this point. CEOs are held responsible for incompetence, dishonesty, and insensitivity to human suffering, demonstrated by frequent and massive layoffs. Destruction caused by this ruthlessness from CEOs has resulted in total devastation of job security on a global basis.

On December 4th, 2010, Vice President Joe Biden said the solution to the financial crisis is jobs, jobs, jobs, and jobs! This is the title of one of the chapters in my *Layoffs & Hope* book, which came out in March 2009 which was almost six months ahead of Vice President's speech.

Fact 6: The Department of Employment Development (EDD) does its best to help people find jobs. However, their budgets were limited, even when jobs were available and plentiful. Imagine if EDD could keep all their employees, and create an alliance with the private sector to reinvent the present job market mechanism. Doing this is a win-win for the employers as well as employees. This office needs either competition (the same way that FedEx provided competition for the US Post Office) or it needs to be totally privatized!

Fact 7: The Internet will be a far more powerful tool than infrastructure development to create, and maintain, productive careers and jobs. This is much cheaper, and can take place right away to put America back to work!

Fact 8: Any tax relief should be given only to companies that recall laid-off workers. This will be a great incentive for employers to create jobs! This will make sure that money circulation improves, too.

Fact 9: The Internet can reduce a great deal of resentment towards government by using instant data. For example, during the President's speech this means that instant and actual data will be used for the next instant and in real-time decisions. The will of the people can flash up on computer screens instantly on any issue. We are talking about instant real data and no filters, no news media analysis, and no expert witness guessing. This is reality-based, real-time, and empowering data for instant decision.

Work Action Plan for the American Economy Regarding Job Creation

1. Stop mass importation of cheap labor under the H1B Visa regulations that were devised for when there was 2% unemployment in many IT and technical sectors, during the height of the dot-com boom and almost full American employment. The H1B Visa in this economy does not make sense during double-digit unemployment.

2. Tabulate a company by company statistics that shows the percentage of layoffs and percentage of American jobs side by side with overseas employment and job creation/destruction, and the percentage of American employees for an American company here in the US. This is a sort of corporation or company version of the FICA score that so many American consumers have been living by, and struggling with some painfully obsolete and false indicators such as FICA. FICA has become so irrelevant as an indicator that some businesses are asking to see the utility bill payment records as a substitute for FICA.

3. Tabulate a company-by-company list of assets kept outside the USA by American companies.

4. Plead with President Clinton to take on the dedicated management of American Economic Recovery/Job Creation. It is highly critical that a person of his experience and stature assists President Obama and his team in this unemployment crisis.

5. Propose flat income-based taxation.

6. Expand the job creation team to include working and dedicated members, equally divided among Republicans and Democrats, of working and unemployed executives and regular employees to meet weekly to develop and then foresee the implementation of:

a. Strategic plans,
b. Tactical plans,
c. Generate blueprints and detailed action items on how to reduce American unemployment by 1% in 90 days. Many American companies have learned that they need to reinvent themselves regularly and repeatedly to survive, and even thrive, in good as well as bad times.
d. Up-to-the-minute status reflected on a transparent and universally visible dashboard.

7. Develop government, major business, small business alliances and partnerships producing practical, nonpolitical actionable advice, ideas, blueprints, and step-by-step action items.

8. Enforce Free Trade with India and China, according to the laws already on the books.

9. Require a set percentage of each product or service manufactured overseas to be done in the US if that product or service is to be sold in the USA.

10. Companies must consider hiring "double zero employees," also known as OOE, similar to OO7 in the movies. These employees will volunteer to work for free, or for a nominal salary, with the employer deducting all taxation and fringe benefits related to each individual employee from their paycheck. This means that companies can no longer use the excuse that they are paying too much tax burden on the employer! The 00E is a win-win scenario that can help many experienced and good employees and cash-strapped companies keep going.

i. Reinvention of the American Labor Union Movement. Better yet, creation of American Labor, Management, and Consumer Union Movement! It is a lose-lose situation that many companies in Silicon Valley were never unionized. A progressive, proactive, and respected labor union could well

146

serve as a checks and balances mechanism, inherent in American democracy and freedom. KGO radio is San Francisco is a shining example of this. In Ronn Owen show, there were guests who talked about how inadequate the food stamps allowance of $4.72 per person per day is. The author of one book actually spent some time in allowing herself that $4.72 per day for breakfast, lunch, and dinner! Can you live on $4.72 per day for food?

11. Adaptation of Starbucks' latest management practices and required employee obligations as one good example for mutual trust and loyalty.

12. American employee and consumer-based "Our Voice Being Heard" letter writing, blogging, emailing, and calling CEOs of companies, institutions, and individuals who are seen to be practicing anti-employment.

13. Public radio and television, as well as private stations, conducting job creation programs similar to their present regular fund-raising programs.

"General Commander" Warren Buffett Declares War on unemployment

When Warren Buffett, a well known multibillionaire, came out and said that he had paid less income tax than his secretary, and that was unfair, he made me one of his fans!

As mentioned before, we need to declare war on unemployment. American businesses and the economy revolve around jobs, jobs, jobs, jobs. It is jobs that create consumer confidence and spending. Consumer spending is what keeps the American economy healthy. I hope that you, too, have realized that without jobs for Americans in America, Americans would have no money to spend and to consume even the basic necessities of life, like bread, and gas for the car.

This was even evident to the Chinese government. They are conducting classes teaching their citizens how to consume and how to become entrepreneurs. The French are encouraging their citizens to learn from Americans and become entrepreneurs. My hat is off to both of them.

Going back to Warren Buffett, he made a huge donation to the Bank of America to prevent that bank, a cornerstone of American economics, from total bankruptcy. This tells me that Warren Buffett has realized that America is fighting in three fronts; Afghanistan, Iraq, and the economic livelihood of Americans. What is by far more important is that he, unlike many others, did not just say something; he did something. Think empowerment; think inspiration; think thinking out of the box, out of the container, and even out of normal wisdom or the prison of the "we have always done this thing, this way," mental malady box! Shatter the glass ceiling! By taking action rather than sitting there and being afraid, we can permit and empower ourselves to help us to reinvent, to re-inspire, regroup, and rethink the impossible! I assure you that 90% of the final success usually follows after taking the first 10% action.

So, in my book, he is just as important as any of our generals who are fighting in Afghanistan and Iraq! He is just as heroic as the military general commanders. Believe me, we need more of them; we need more Democrat economic general commanders, and need more Republicans! The other economic general commander that I know of is Howard Schultz, of

Starbucks.

Do you believe that this general financial crisis is something that American government and American government alone can solve? Are you of the belief that we, as Americans, should sit in our living rooms and watch an unending debate about how to solve it on TV? I do not think that that will solve the problem. We need to take action, just like Warren Buffett did.

The American economy runs on jobs fuel; the American economy runs on consumer spending; American life revolves around Americans not losing their houses to outrageous executive salaries and rampant reckless mismanagement.

It's time for Americans to act like Warren Buffet did! Of course, if you happen to have a few million dollars in some empty coffee can, then do something for all of us and spend that money, or part of it! However, most likely you are just like us. You are barely making ends meet; your 401K plan has become 01K since it has 0 dollars in it; you are unemployed, or unhappily employed; you have no job security; and your kids will definitely have a lower standard of living than you did, and this makes you depressed and ashamed! As a volunteer who has worked with the unemployed, I know this feeling of bitter hopelessness, sadness, self-doubt, and self-hate. I experienced all these when I was laid off for the first time, in 1984! Most Americans want to work and be productive; most Americans want to respect themselves and be productive members of society. However, when some CEO edict comes down that "you're fired," the awful impact is such that they, in the American hard work ethic, internalize what was the direct result of CEO mismanagement and blame themselves for it. They, who are victims of latest massive and frequent layoffs, hold themselves, and themselves alone, responsible for this. This kills not only the person's humanity, but it also causes of billions, or even trillions of dollars' worth of loss. The loss of face in some Chinese-American, Japanese-Americans and other ancient cultures alone can cause devastating and permanent damage to their humanity.

The feeling was best summarized by a friend, after being fired from a major corporation. "Bruce I'm damaged goods! I will never find another job!"

Unfortunately, in spite all my efforts, this self-imposed

sentence ended up being a self-fulfilling predicament. He never found another job, while his brother supported him and his family. However, this will not happen to us. We will succeed and we will thrive.

In my thirty-two years of work in Silicon Valley, I have yet to see any of these layoffs work in the long-term for the company, employees, customers, or even the stockholders. It was mismanagement that got us into this crisis, and it is management that will get us out of this.

I would like to see more economic general commanders step forward. For example, I would like Mr. Brian Moynihan of Bank of America to do the best he can to restore American jobs and pride. I would like Mr. Fredrick Smith of FedEx start a new company called JobEx.

In the final analysis, the solution is with you and I, as Americans.

Let's designate Columbus Day, October 12 2012, as the Great American day of raising our Voice! Let us in a legal, peaceful, and constructive way tell all who are willing to hear that we need and want jobs!

Let's prepare pickets signs and get protest permits with a sign that reads, "JOBS NOW!" This is as American as apple pie, even though the pie pan is stamped "Made in China!" Let's go to streets, let's conduct peaceful sit-ins in banks, major corporations, and small businesses. Since it was on Columbus Day that America was discovered, let's rediscover our Americanism and American economy by breaking our silence. During the later parts of the Vietnam War there was a big bulletin in Madison, Wisconsin that said to parents and citizens, "Your Silence is Killing Us!"

Get it off your chest. After all, this is America and we can say and do anything, as the Honorable George Schultz, former Secretary of State, told me! American voices, or silence, will be heard! Please note that I am strongly proposing a peaceful and lawful demonstration in a productive way. I am proposing solutions in a constructive way to be brought to the attention of companies.

APPENDIX E
"General Commander" Professor David Cheriton of Stanford University Starts American Googelar Production Line Innovation Manufacturing (GP-LIM)!

In an interview with Matt Frei of BBC, Professor David Cheriton told Matt that he encouraged the two founders of Google to start their company – Google – with the basic idea of putting all the information in the world in one suitcase. It's rumored that Prof. Cheriton was able to give them a venture capital check right on the grass in his yard.

Everybody is either upset or envious of China as being the materials manufacturing capitalist superpower of the world. I am not! Mr. B., in *What Color is Your Parachute?* Makes a clear statement that has served me extremely well for the twenty or more years that I have been his follower! He says that we have to "learn, unlearn, learn, and learn to be competitive!" I'm sure that Chinese business and government have read an implemented Mr. B.'s motto!

Since I have lived and worked in Silicon Valley for more than thirty years, I can guarantee you that American prowess is not in material manufacturing, but in innovation! This is recognized around the world and it has been challenged, unsuccessfully, many times, by many nations. Even the flood of new arrivals from India and China (hopefully the next generation of productive and patriotic Americans) has not been able to imitate or reinvent the American innovation secret of pioneering and reinventing new materials, intellectual ideas and patents, and globe-changing social networking or other things.

Imagine, a production line run by Prof. Cheriton, starting in Stanford, where each day, in factory style, new ideas are studied, reviewed, and finally recommended to a big group of venture capitalists waiting to give them the needed seed money, or make major investments.

When my software and hardware team was working on development of ZSCAN80, we did just about as much material and innovation manufacturing as I sadly see go into even some of the most successful products. ZSCAN80 was introduced to the market in 1982! In the twenty-nine years that have passed, there has been a minimal amount of advancement in innovation that is integrated into products. Twitter, Google, Apple, and others are exceptions. However, the sad truth is that most of the effort seems to go into making a faster and/or cheaper mouse trap, and not a fully-integrated product that captures and caters to digital humanity's needs.

Many of us were trained to believe that old capitalism had to have a misery index. It trained us to accept that a 4% unemployment rate and the pains that imposed on the community and society, as well as its financial loss, was just a part of the way things were supposed to be.

It must be just as important to consider human capital as much as we consider the materials capital in our future decisions. With Internet technology, there is no need to forecast a market segment. We can use sophisticated simulation software to almost immediately measure the impact of things. We do not need to wait for marketing postures, advertising campaigns, and guesswork. We turn the knob on a product by 2%, and we can measure instantly its effect on price elasticity, market share percentage figures, and even the percentage of additional unemployment. It's no surprise that we can get this data from Internet, instantly.

You might recall that I had several paragraphs on the vicious cycle that layoffs have created in Silicon Valley, and continue to produce in the entire world. However, double-digit unemployment and the rampant rise of poor people among us attests to the fact that at some point there will be a boiling point; at some point, people will not be able to take this anymore; at some point, there will be a backlash.

My prayers and hopes are that if there is a backlash or revolt, I hope that it will be ethical, peaceful, and civil. At some point, so many Americans will lose their homes to foreclosure that they start to raise their voice. My hope is that that voice be in the form of emails, blogs, Facebook, twitter, and www.youtube.com clips that share a point of view, proposes a constructive solution, and asks for the readers to accept or reject the solution. This gives ultimate power to the "Like" button in Facebook.

Based on our combined experience of a century or so, the most powerful and immediate tool America has is innovation and invention. Remember that there is strong belief that savage American Mother Nature is what made America courageous enough to be a superpower. Now we need to take all the hardships of the Afghanistan and Iraq wars, and the third front that is the economic war, to be courageous and innovative to make America an ultra-power. The words of my first physical trainer, "Bruce if you say you cannot do something, then that 'cannot' will rule your life and imprison you so you will never do it! If you cannot do a mile, do half a mile, a quarter of mile, or even one step. And think what it is that you can do right now and go do it!" He should know. He was a champion in his country of origin's Olympics team, with a Ph. D. in Sports Psychology.

At some point, American citizens and consumers will raise their voices and say, "Mr. or Madam CEO, if you recall some of the employees that were laid off from your company, we will buy more of the products and services offered by your company." Mutual loyalty and trust is a two-way street.

If I was the CEO at eBay, and based on what I learned working there as a senior consultant, I could have integrated and powered up Skype with the eBay auction engine to provide a colossal product and service to help human beings who are unemployed or underemployed. Each time I went to the C-Level executive meeting, I could not help but wonder what a big opportunity was being lost in not knowing how to continue the innovation engine, and not the just the auction engine, at eBay. Skype has by far more innovative prowess in it than was ever realized. I sincerely hope that the new owners of Skype, Microsoft Corporation, can be proactive and put that to great use in serving humanity. After all, it's the innovation engine that will make America the global ultra-power that it can become. It's not cheap labor making cheap imitation products.

Greed, for the lack of a better word, is good; in fact it is great! Therefore to make lots and lots of money, companies have to unlearn, relearn, and learn and learn almost each day to be proactively profitable by doing philanthropy. The giant company Google's motto is "Do no harm!" We can go one step further; we need to do what is best for the customer, and the customer will knock at our door to buy our products. Notice the alarming difference from the days when a new mousetrap was supposed to bring buyers to our doors.

I do want companies and CEOs to make zillions of dollars, and they can. To do that, even in this most God-awful down market, is to think out of box, think huge, and think innovation and humanity! Brazil is an example of how this can happen.

The new way to make money, or monetize, as in the slang in Silicon Valley for making money from a product or service, is to give it out for free!

Yes, to give it out for free! Google or Twitter do not charge you anything for using their service. Add to that the adage invented by yours truly; "The best way to sell something on the Internet is to sell it for free! That is what the online customers are telling us; that I am not buying it unless it is free!"

Suppose Microsoft comes out and says, you can use Skype just as reliably integrated as Microsoft Word to conduct, for free, your business from your home office. Suppose that some of Prof. Chariton's Stanford University students invent a new innovation engine that make it just as effortless for you to sit at home and use Skype to do 90% of your work, as you did when you physically showed up for work in an office in a brick and mortar building. Before you object that this idea already exists and it was put to work years ago, let me tell you that it is not. It is not because it is not integrated into office products, and the digital humanity part of it is lacking

.

Our country and the entire globe are trying to cope with a global financial crisis. Does it not stand to reason that in addition to huge efforts by our government, President, Republicans, and Democrats, we do another effort from highly innovative angle?

Imagine, there are 700,000 post office employees that are

working each day in an industry that is already obsolete. Imagine, there are thousands of American soldiers and their families who risked their lives and sacrificed a great deal to serve their country. These battle-hardened soldiers need to be treated with the best our country can afford to reabsorb them into being productive and happy members of society.

We can indeed do these and more! As the Six Million Dollar Man said, "We have the technology!" We have Internet technology; we have what we have learned from bitter lessons of the global financial crisis. We, as Americans, will reinvent our business and economy to be that ultra-power that we can be!

"General Commander" of FedEx Duplicates FedEx to Save American Jobs (JobEx)!

This business plan was discussed with several Silicon Valley venture capitalists in June of 2011. It has kept its value-added vision as the day it was presented to Dr. Eric Benhemou, CEO and Chairman of the Board at 3COM and others.

I print this business plan exactly as it was. I have that much confidence in it! It will save and create jobs!

JobEx

- $2.4 Trillion productivity loss annually at 4% "ideal" unemployment
- US unemployment benefits are inferior compared to Europeans
- Average unemployment duration of about one year
- No innovations in job search sites during the last ten years
- About 50% of employees not happy with their careers
- Employment Development Department (EDD) severely under-resourced
- EDD is like US Post Office (USPO), and JobEx is reinvention of EDD similar to FedEx's reinvention of USPO

JobEx, FedEx Vs. USPO, EDD

Presently, as a result of the global financial crisis (GFC), California is experiencing about 12% unemployment. Compared to Europe, the unemployed American gets almost no help in finding a job. Therefore, there is an immense opportunity to create a new enterprise that fulfills this humanitarian and financially lucrative gap.

The Employment Development Department (EDD) is seriously under-resourced; EDD provides inadequate job search support; EDD's function is almost entirely limited to printing unemployment checks. To save operating costs, EDD is considering outsourcing their Call Center to India. Thus there will be even less services for the unemployed.

EDD inadequacies results in long unemployment periods for the workforce that is capable and eager and to work, and work immediately. Much of the human suffering, foreclosures, and lifetime savings loss can be avoided if JobEx is created.

As the *Layoffs & Hope* book establishes, frequent and massive layoffs have created a higher share of toxic work environments, conducive to fear of sudden job loss that undermines mutual trust and loyalty, which is the foundation of employee job satisfaction and company profitability.

By doing the old-fashioned human resource functions on a human-to-human trust (H2HT) basis, and using the latest technology, JobEx will provide a high ROI and will be an innovative and well-respected endeavor.

Using the latest technology from JobNob (www.jobnob.com), time-tested and effective processes from HP Consulting (http://www.hpconsulting.com), H2H enabling tools such as Skype (www.skype.com), and bookkeeping systems such as Sabre Reservations (www.sabre.com), JobEx will be the ultimate online career management, even bigger than eBay is to auction industry.

An eCommerce can go online in less than thirty days. Within sixty days, a beta functional eCommerce site can be launched. Within ninety days, a million subscribers are projected. This is similar to people trying to find job offers (on an action-based system), just like Google is used to find general information (on an information and data-based system).

As Mr. Razban, author of *Layoffs & Hope*, has indicated, the workplace of the future will be drastically different. Let's take advantage of this immense financial bonanza. After all, he wrote the book on this subject and *Layoffs & Hope* has been at times the #4 most popular www.amazon.com download in the careers and psychology sections.

Also, his service to the White House as a community leader in Silicon Valley and intensive work on this subject with many C-Level Executives, and the resulting report indicated that a JobEx enterprise is needed, is humanitarian, and will have awesome ROI.

Mr. Razban got an A in Stanford University Business School Continuing Education for the JobEx proposal. It is rumored that Mr. Fredrick Smith got a C on his FedEx proposal in the same Business Class, titled, *How to Start a Successful Start Up.*

JobEx fundamentals:

- Universal Uniform Resumes (UUR)
- Virally Marketable Tested Skills (VMTS)
- Uniform Job Requirements (UJB)
- JobNob and eLance processes
- Assignment of Human Job Expert Guide (HJEG)
- Online Human-to-Human Staff Meeting (H2HSM)

- Roadmap, Strategy, Action Item, Planning daily online w/HJEG)
- Employee and employer certified, Experience Score Card (ESC)

JobEx high level modus operandi:

- Heavy automation of what optimizes profits, and humanization of what has to be H2H to increase productivity
- Harnessing existing chaotic systems and processes and exploiting Mr. Razban's Workplace of the Future (WPF) to produce massive success on the wreckage of existing state of the prior art

JobEx Potential Customers:

- US Government
- HP Consulting
- Robert Half Employment Agency
- Manpower Employment Agency
- Management Recruiters
- Major Corporations
- Start-ups

JobEx Road Map:

- ECommerce prototype 34 days: Production eCommerce website 62 days; 1,000,000 subscriptions, 95 days.

JobEx Monetization:

- Flat, onetime 10% of Annual base salary, or 5% of hourly contractor/consultant hourly pay for all hours

Special Thanks:
- Stanford University Business School
- www.HPshopping.com and www.HPcosulting.com executives, especially Erik Lessing
- Anil Uberoi, CMO
- Eric Wheels, Former General Manager of Management

Recruiters International (MRI)

- IICON Corporation executives

In Memory of:

- Bobbie Bogue, a pioneering former Zilog colleague who invented "Adobe Premier" on a shoestring budget, twelve years before Adobe marketed their version

REFERENCES:

- Job Creation Proposal submitted to the White House
- Stanford University Business Plan on Jobs
- *Layoffs & Hope*, Bruce B. Razban, Amazon.com
- ProMatch, Connect, and Nova, Sunnyvale, CA
- *What Color is Your Parachute?* Amazon.com and other books and seminars by Richard Bolles (Mr. B.)
- Extensive YouTube, Radio Talk Shows, and published articles by Mr. Razban as a career coach, management consultant, and consultant with 32 years of experience

Similarities between Present Unemployment Situation and Vietnam War

Unfortunately, the Vietnam War is forgotten. During that seemingly never-ending war, there came a point that the "most trusted American" newsman and CBS anchor, Walter Cronkite, stood up and said that the Vietnam War was wrong. That was the turning point, and the beginning of the end for that unpopular war.

Company after company lay off hundreds and thousands of employees and nobody raises his or her voice. Nobody buys a single share of the company and then goes to the stockholder's meeting and ask the CEO and Board of Directors about why so many jobs were killed and tells them there is a better way! Why nobody buys a share of these companies' stocks and goes to shareholder meeting to tell the CEO "Stop these layoffs! Please use my business plan so you will not need to lay off employees just to make your company look good on the surface!"

Like a group of sheep, we politely pick up some empty carton box, put our belongings in it, shamefully and quietly assume that it was our fault, and leave the premises.

Another company buys the competition and nobody says anything. Then half of the hard-working employees are branded surplus, and they, too, are sent like sheep to pick up their belongings and "leave the premises." These affected employees are then deposited in "no longer works here," to be instantly invisible.

Then some smart-aleck CEO says that he cannot create products cheap enough here, so he has to offshore hundreds and thousands of jobs. John Palmers of Cisco System, who is a well-respected and liked Silicon Valley CEO, said these exact words to Leslie Sthal in a 60 Minutes interview. These were painful words for me to hear from this outstanding CEO. It was not that long after that that Cisco, in an article in San Jose *Mercury-News* announced that their revenue would be going down farther than they had previously thought! I wish I could talk to Mr. Palmers face to face, Human to Human (H2H). I am convinced that I can convince him that there are better ways and more effective ways than layoffs. This reminds me of Barbara Boxer's statement to former HP CEO Carley Fiorina, "Please have a heart! Your company has laid off 30,000 employees during your watch!"

Then some other company is caught off-guard for bad

management, and to make the books look good, bingo!, hundreds or thousands of jobs are vanished, along with kid's college plans, and their ability to have a productive and happy life. Again, nobody says anything.

Yahoo releases the latest email with several problems, and nobody really says anything. Carol Bartz is finally fired, but she was offended that it was done during a phone call.

We have gone totally crazy! The total truth is that this is a radically different world with much different business and economy rules. This is a reinvented American Global Capitalism that is in charge.

Eureka! Remember that at the beginning of this book we were trying to find out whose fault this awful economy and business is. The list of villains, at the beginning, included government, management, CEOs, Boards of Director, and even consumers! Also, please remember that I was also trying to find out whether there was a conspiracy. My list included Republicans and Democrats as potential head villains. Perhaps in these dire economic conditions, according to the HP school of management, it does not make any difference. We're in this together, and let's use win-win methods to find a solution. So, without further ado, let me tell you that all the above potential villains can now use this outstanding opportunity and become global heroes. They can become global heroes by:

- Unlearning, relearning, learning, and re-relearning to use the reinvented global American Capitalism instead of the old materials-only-based Capitalism.

- Use fantastic new technology like Twitter, FaceBook, and other technology in the real-time Internet to minimize waste and inefficiencies and maximize prosperity, using proactive profitable philanthropy to put America back to work! I guess that our research has come up with one of the lines from the Forest Gump movie that said, "Stupid is What Stupid Does!" Remember that it is the working Americans who can revive American economy by spending as good consumers did, and will do again.

- The most powerful agent in this war for creating more jobs are those previously thought to be villains, such as American Democrats, or Republicans, etc., who, like Warren Buffett and new CEOs of your own life and company, can bring the almost dead American economy back to life.

It seems from a distance that everyone has his or her total truth, and no one is interested in the *real* total truth.

Democrats announce a plan, only to be shot down by Republicans, and Republicans propose something that is deemed totally unacceptable by Democrats. Congress has lost its appeal. Unfortunately, at this point in time Americans, emotionally or financially, just do not care to trust almost anyone anymore.

Let's designate this coming Columbus Day (October 12th, 2011, which happens to be my birthday) as the Great American Speaking Up, and even boycott buying products and services from companies that have killed jobs.

STOP ORDER!

We think that with all due respect and credit, our government and politicians are and will continue do the best they can to help the job crisis. We are using the word crisis carefully here. Double digit unemployment, and the fact that many people are underemployed, is indeed a national American crisis.

In one of the examples in the book, I talked about the situation at Plantronics, Inc. where there were problems with a mechanical part, and we had to decide to scrap $3,000 worth of parts. However, prior to fixing the crisis, we had to issue a stop order. A stop order alerts all departments that there has been a problem and we just cannot go about our jobs the way we used to. We need to fix this problem before things will go back to normal. The stop orders were usually printed on dark red paper to grab attention. This dark red color made the paper look as if it was soaked in blood! Going back to the national joblessness and financial crisis, we also mentioned before that this awful crisis is basically a business and economic problem. In addition, we took the position that, unlike the weather, this Global Financial Crisis can be managed, and therefore fixed.

Thus, let's issue a stop order as follows:

- Banks and other financial institutions: Voluntarily stop all foreclosures immediately – for 30 days, 60, or 90 days - as there's already a glut of houses on the market, threatening to destroy the fabric of our society.
- We're talking about foreclosures of houses that people are living in.
- Many people, including myself, had their FICA Score totally destroyed, directly or indirectly, as a result of the Global Financial Crisis. In many cases, people who had never been less than perfect, resulting from decades of paying their bills on time got a low score for being unemployed for a year or two, or even more.

- Private Sector: Stop all layoffs for the same period, as above.
- Assign volunteer experts from Harvard, Stanford, and MIT as well as the London School of Economics, Sorbonne, Technion, etc. to be focused on formulating a solution.

Please note, I am not talking regulations, laws, or any other kind of government edicts. I am asking, for example, that Mr. Brian Moynihan, CEO of Bank of America, to stop foreclosures unilaterally in the name of Bank of America founder, Mr. Giannini. This is based on the fact that after the massive San Francisco earthquake, Mr. Giannini provided badly needed banking services out of a makeshift office and lent people money based on a handshake. I can almost guarantee it that if Bank of America did this it will make a lot more money, since it has respected mutual trust and loyalty. Americans might decide to close their accounts in HSBC, who had decided to lose its trust in America; layoff thousands of employees, and move their operations elsewhere, as if America was not good enough for them.

Based on my thirty years of experience, layoffs do not work in the long term, and they are devastating to company productivity.

Due to the massive nature of this unemployment situation and the fact that President Clinton has just recently said that "since I am not in the office any more, I can do things that are unpopular!" What President Clinton was referring to were things that were desperately needed to be done, but were not being done. He would be an excellent person to be begged, enticed, or encouraged to volunteer his almost full time effort, and leading the American economic reinvention and fix. I'll never forget that during his presidency we were doing well financially, and that he was loved in the Nova organization. Nova is a volunteer organization in Silicon Valley, supported by the industry, which helped many people get jobs by retraining. President Clinton's picture was framed and on the Nova walls, showing him during his visit to Nova in Silicon Valley.

In addition to this, many volunteer unemployed people will gladly be eager to help, as well.

APPENDIX I
Living and Working in Constant Crisis, and Unemployment

The weekend before the tenth anniversary of the 9/11 the terrorist attack, I heard three things on the radio that shook me up. The first was from Dave, one of my favorite news analysts, on KCBS radio is San Francisco. "What if Osama Ben Laden's terror target was not just those people that he killed during the Twin Tower attacks?" he announced, alarmingly. I was getting full of rage for hearing this, since this exact thing was what I had suspected, yet had not dared to verbalize. Considering that the first truck attack was against innocent people in a trade center, I had thought that Osama not only wanted to kill people, but he also wanted to destroy America as a world trade economy and power. Dave went on with his strong and insightful analysis by saying, "Osama's goal was to destroy the American economy, and thus bring on the Global Financial Crisis!" To back this up, he referred to some evidence found after Osama's capture and death in Pakistan.

I was sick to my stomach! Conceivably, this is indeed highly probable. I mean probable in Osama's intentions, thoughts, planning, and execution!

A few hours later, I called Dr. Bill Wattenberg's radio talk show, broadcast from the KGO Radio. Dr. Bill is an engineer and scientist by training, who has a wealth of knowledge on almost any subject, and has a huge following.

My question to him was simple. I asked, "Dr. Bill, we have heard about what the government and politicians are supposed to do to deal with mass unemployment. However, the more important thing, for me and many other middle class Americans, is how we can find and/or maintain a job in this turbulent job market."

He answered this question with his typical insight, care, and up-to-date information! "Bruce, there are about 14 million unemployed Americans. Then there are about 8 million underemployed Americans who will jump to a better job the minute they are given a chance. So, unfortunately, I'm sorry to tell you that it will be a long time before the unemployed can get a job!" Then, in voice that clearly conveyed sadness and empathy, he added, "Bruce, I would take any job, and I mean *any* job, that I can get if I was in your situation!"

I had listened to his program for many years, and I had always been impressed, but this time it went above and beyond that. I will be his fan for a very long time to come.

In an interview with a colleague who had managed to hang on to his job all along in these turbulent times, I was amazed to hear what he had to say. He said, "Bruce, we were forced to apply for our own old jobs. Then there was a re-organization that did not add any value and added a great deal of confusion. Then there was a layoff, then the CEO got fired and they brought a replacement who decided to fire several of the best employees in his first week, and bring in his cronies from his previous job. Then there was this hiring binge, bringing Indians, fresh from India, who were given the jobs before they even left India; then there was overt job discrimination against older employees; then there was about sixty to seventy percept of our daily work that was politically-based and added absolutely no value. On top of that, there is no job security; nobody cares, and nobody trusts anyone else! This, in turn, brings productivity and innovation to a miserably low level! The manager, being from a third world country, does not keep his/her word; consulting fees are reduced at will by the employer, and assignments are almost impossible to do. Our group manager, who is from a third world country, runs the group as if America is already a third world country."

Another friend and colleague told me to look at the company telephone book; there are only 5% American sounding last names, or less. By mass importation of cheap labor, off-shoring, and other destructive practices, we have created massive global imbalances and security risks. While we respect both India and China for their monumental accomplishments, we would like to warn them of an impending socio-economic imbalance that will destroy the fabric of their communities as a result of massive cheap labor exports from them and imports for us.

In a documentary on Public TV, the theme was that America had to have tamed some unfathomable and savage Mother Nature disasters just to become the America that stood up among all nations. While these disasters were as bad as they could be, the severity of them was a good impetus for America and Americans to gather courage to build the greatest nation on earth on top and beyond all these potentially devastating disasters. This American creation history parallels two other nations. Holland, for instance, is country built on land claimed from the turbulent North Sea, inch by inch. Israel is another example where a modern nation was reinvented from the ashes of the Holocaust in a land that was a desert. Israel, with help from America, made the desert bloom. Incidentally, as a Director, I had travelled all around the world on business. In most places, as an American, I had been subject of envy, dislike, or mistrust. I had been lectured to as being a citizen of country that wastes a lot, takes advantage of other countries, and that I really had to be ashamed of myself and country. Israel was one of the few strong and heartwarming exceptions. In almost all cases, they seemed to be genuinely interested in the latest news about America; they wanted to know how Americans really lived; they wanted me to know that they liked or actually loved America, and they dreamed of someday being like America. To many Israelis, America and Americans are bigger than life!

Diane Feinstein, in a CNN interview with Wolfe Blitzer a few days before the tenth anniversary of the 911 terrorist attack, pointed out that America, like Israel, lives in a dangerous world. She added that just like the Israelis, we need to learn to live our full life even under these circumstances. "We need to be on the alert at all times in our airports and wherever we are."

This reminded me of one of my business trips to Israel. I had barely settled in my hotel room when the phone rang. "Sir, there is a telegram for you that says urgent. Would you want us to bring it your room?"

The telegram said that my dad had suddenly passed away, almost an hour after I arrived in Israel. Unfortunately, this being the height of tourist season, British Airways next flight that they could get me a seat on was the next day. I could not wait. I checked out of the hotel less than twelve hours after I had checked in. When I got to the airport, I was surprised to see that my name was on a list. The attractive airport security officer who had carefully and quickly checked my suitcase told me that the hotel had called, and that I had their condolences. She added that the Ben Gurion Airport staff would do all they could do to help me fly back home as soon as possible. "Sorry, sorry, almost all flights are full. However, there is an El Al Israeli Airline flight to Vienna that is full too, but we will treat you as if you were a member of our military and put you on that flight."

This was what the airport manager told me. As I was waiting to see if I could get on that flight, I heard my name on the speakers. Without hesitation, I ran to the ticket counter.

"Mr. Razban, we managed to get you on that El Al flight, and put you on a connecting flight to London, and then direct to San Francisco on British Airways, at no extra charge to you! We are sorry that this happened to you on your trip to Israel. However, we sincerely hope that your next trip will be a happy one. After all, we take good care of our tourists!"

After hearing this, I said, "I'm really grateful for this VIP treatment." Then I added that I'm a nobody, and I felt a bit embarrassed to see this. "However, I'm very grateful!"

After a pause, the airport staff told me, "Sir, you are not a nobody. You are an American, and America is our best friend and ally!"

At that point, and after having conquered my crisis for that moment, I was almost ready to take a nap when I was told that I needed to rush to the gate and board the El Al flight to Vienna. The flight was absolutely full. I noticed that there were several rows occupied by a Christian Pilgrimage Tour Group to Jerusalem. They seemed to be happy, and were delighted for having made this pilgrimage. Across the aisle, there was a rabbi traveling with his son. Soon after hearing that my dad had passed away, he offered to help me tell Kaddish, which is the Jewish prayer for the deceased. The flight attendant ushered us to the back of the airplane and gave us enough time to pay my last respects to my father.

A high-ranking priest from the Christian group later on came to my seat to tell me that they had heard from the rabbi that my father had passed away and they were praying for me and my family to have the strength and patience to go on living, even with this tragedy. "I would like to remind you of Psalm 23 my son." This was what I heard from the priest before he had to rush back to his seat, as the plane had already started its descent and "Fasten Seat Belts" signs were glaringly reminding us to prepare for the landing. A part of Psalm 23 says, "Even in the valley of death, we have no fear!"

Have no fear! I think that it must be the operating set of words in the American life these days. One of the promises of many twelve-step programs is that the fear of financial insecurity will be removed from us. The wording of this promise is intense and yet delicate; it does not promise that financial insecurity will be removed from us, it just says that the fear of such thing will be removed so we can freely live our lives and do the best we can to cope and even thrive even in a crisis.

APPENDIX J
What, Exactly, is Meant by Value-Added and Triple-Decker Career Bus?

Let me give you an example of what value-added means. When I became a director at Zilog, Inc., I was assigned a highly recommended and hard working, dedicated, and extremely helpful admin.

She always showed up and left early; she diligently stamped every piece of documentation and correspondence that was sent to me. Those days email was not quite invented yet. She had this difficult and heavy "Date and Department Stamper" that she used to stamp with. This was such a heavy tool that at times would give her shoulder pain. She made sure that every birthday for my sixty-eight employee organization was observed by buying cakes and making sure there was fresh coffee. She made sure all my meetings had conference rooms assigned to them, since we were in stiff competition with other departments in the same building.

While all of the above work was needed and I was grateful for it, she did not even stop and think that what she was doing could be done by a clerk. Of course, the clerk would make a lot less, and the quality of his/her work would not be as great. However, the value of what she was contributing kept diminishing.

I understood her well, because we both had the same Puritan work ethics. However, I decided to be fair with her and tell her the risk she was taking, since the value of her work to the company was getting less and less.

She agreed with me, but was not ready to do something about this. We both seemed to have the American diseases of talking and talking, so we did not do anything to solve the problem.

During one of our extremely well-planned group meetings, I announced to the entire group that since my admin had done such a great work, I had signed her up for an introductory course to email that was being conducted by HP. She said thanks in a subdued voice, and told all of us that she really was grateful. Then, as if she had been hit over the head by a baseball bat, she went to the back of the room and was somewhat quiet.

After the meeting was over, she knocked at my office door, and said "Bruce this course costs too much money, and I cannot accept it. Besides, if I am gone two days for this the entire department will fall apart! Please let me see if I can cancel it, if the cancellation does not cost too much." I convinced her that the company and she herself owed her this educational training. She left, grudgingly.

She came back tired and demoralized at the beginning. "Bruce, there were so many smart admins there that I was horrified. I did not sleep well the night before I went, and did not get much sleep while I was taking it!"

Frankly, I was worried that the next Monday after the weekend, she'd show up to work with a resignation! However, after a few days, she had become the "Go-to person for the email!" She seemed to start to enjoy her new duty, along with the seven percent salary increase, to help others learn HP email.
Soon after that, I sent her to a seminar for Executive Admins. That increased her "Added-Value" immensely.

Many people become so complacent that they do not realize that we constantly need to increase our value in our career and work.

A friend was a flight engineer for Boeing 707 jets for an airline. He knew that he would soon be replaced with automation, but he did not do much about it. Then one day, he got his pink shock of getting a pink layoff notice. He could have trained; he could have gone to classes that were free for his education. But, he insisted that he was happy with his work and the company was happy, and that was all that was important. He suffered several months of unemployment before he had to downshift and get a desk job in that airline.

An old colleague used to take pride in being the CPO, that is, Corporate Politics Officer in the company that he had worked for many years. He knew everyone, and had learned how to influence them to get things done. "Bruce about eighty percent of what people do in big corporations is politics!" was his pet statement.

One day he got fired for no reason. It took him several

years to learn a new skill-set and earn less than what he was making at the company all those years. "Bruce, the worst thing was that after I was fired and after I had been gone for several months, an ex-colleague told me that nobody remembered me and the work was getting done after I had left as if I had never been there!"

The triple-decker bus is one of the main points of this book. This concept helps us to have work during the toughest and most horrible and turbulent times in our economy.

Based on my 32 years of experience as well those of many people from London School of Economics, Stanford University, National Semiconductor University, Sorbonne, and others it has become obvious that we need to have more than one career. In fact, it is proven in our experience that we need three careers, and thus the concept of triple-decker bus.

The triple-decker concept is based on the following:

- We really need to have three careers instead of just one.
    - ✓ The primary career is what we are trained for, and the one that we have had some experience at. It might be the job that we do with our minds. For example, it is senior technical and management consultant.
    - ✓ Then there is the old standby career or job. In my case, that was selling cars and tutoring.
    - ✓ Then there are desperation jobs, these are jobs like delivering pizza, or in my case working at Fry's Electronics, selling.
- Since there is very little or no job security these days, one has to:
    - ✓ Constantly look for that next job as a safeguard against months, or even years, of unemployment, in the event of sudden job loss.

172

- ✓ Constantly network so I can be hired quickly in the event of a sudden job loss.
- ✓ Constant unlearning, relearning, and learning and learning to make sure one has certifiable and marketable skills to be rehired quickly.
- ✓ Constantly refresh your knowledge by studying www.youtube.com clips as well as www.google.com to keep yourself totally updated.
- ✓ Call and go to lunch or coffee with previous colleagues and friends who are working in the same career path that you are.
- ✓ Take as many classes as you can in commuter and community colleges.
- ✓ In addition, you might want to hire a tutor to help you come up to speed on subjects that you are not as confident as you like to be.

- Incorporation Libration teaches us that the best thing to do is to create a one-person company, based on our strengths, and incorporate it quickly, get a business license, and go into business for ourselves.
- Contact LegalZoom and/or other similar companies to help you incorporate yourself.
- By having a company of your own, you will feel more and more confident that a sudden job loss will not make you suffer that much.
- As much as steady job's paycheck is supposed to make you feel secure, this is no longer the case. You must always have a backup job to go to.
- Remember, the most important is that in the even

of a sudden job you do not go without a job for a long time.

- In my own case, my writing as well as selling cars is the obvious standby jobs. However, I have opened another option lately. This option is being a visiting professor at DeVry University/ Keller Graduate School of Management as well as other universities or commuter colleges.
- Since teaching is my passion, I have also been teaching students in the 7th grade as well a smart student who is determined to get perfect score in SAT!
- Along those lines, I am getting ready to teach some high schools with ADD. This will be a privilege.

- The future of work is like cottage industries; no big huge companies and big buildings; no hundreds or thousands of people working for the same big company. A one-person company run from a home office that creates a value-add service or product.

- In the mean time, I just visited Fry's Electronics and our local Macy's store to make sure that they are hiring. This will be just in case I have to work on a desperation basis.
- Please note that I really loved and enjoyed working at Fry's before. That income is one of the most cherished incomes that I have ever had.

APPENDIX K
Rolling in the Deep

Rolling in the Deep is one of Adel's songs that has sold millions. As she was preparing this CD, people must surely have told her that CDs do not sell any more; you will not make money from it, etc. etc. Like a wet blanket, her best friends and managers, with the best of intensions, were telling her what they knew.

Adel decided to make the CD and put all she had to give to it!

She was like a one woman band; she was like a one person company who knew what was needed, and she made it. This young and empowered lady from North London deserves all the credit that she can get. She had enough courage to do what she was best at; give it all her focus and humanly power. The result is history. She will win many awards.

As things are getting worse and worse in the market, and as people are finding that there are no good jobs to be had, the idea of creating your own job and company gets more and more traction. Just like an old saying that the more things change the more they stay the same holds here.

In the beginning, it was the owners who managed their company. They did not have to bring in an outsider to take care of their money and company. Now, we are going back to that old and great idea. By incorporation libration, we are encouraging you to be that one man, or one woman, company!

Find what you are best at, and what you really like to do. Take training or use your lifetime experience to find a marketable and certifiable job. You can learn what a CEO does, quickly, and you will be doing that in no time at all.

This book tells you that we all need to have three careers instead of just one. This is what elucidated and vividly showcased in the triple-decker bus idea.

If anything, massive and frequent layoffs will continue in these turbulent economic times.

By having followed examples given in this book, we hope that you have constructed your career triple-decker bus and have revved up your engine. Just having the assurance that you have options, and can be successful beyond any imagination, will help you cope and thrive!

Companies that are interested in really serving their

community; companies that have the motto of "do no evil" as Google did; companies that practice the best and more pure form of profits as "Proactive, Profitable, and Philanthropy" these are companies that will succeed.

Imagine what our world can become if we reinvent ourselves and use the power of reinvented American Global Capitalism! Sky, or for that matter our galaxy's vast empty sky that is above it, will be the limit!

To follow some of the lyrics, "We could have had it all!" And, we will too!

One way to have it all in the work life is to fortify our skill set and our job search so much that we are not caught by long periods of being unemployed, underemployed, or unhappily employed. We can do this without scarifying our entire life for work.

In many of my graduate management classes I have asked my students to write down where they and their careers would like to be thirty years later. Almost always this question brings back the response that says "We really have not ever thought that far. We cannot tell where we will be one or five years from now let alone thirty!" And, almost in most cases, I tell them about my own experience that one day I really realized that it had been thirty years since I had started working. Along with that realization there was the deep regret that I had not planned my career and my life to have everything that I would have wanted to have by the time that I had worked thirty years.

Even with this I find my students have a hard time doing this critically important task for themselves. Yet, they have no problem doing this "strategic planning" for companies that we use to do our case studies. They quickly make a captivating vision, mission statement, and strategic plan.

A comprehensive study of about twenty of my colleagues

quickly revealed that the most successful people where those who had managed to create a three-in-one career, or in another word a triple-decker bus for their career.

They had their main career, as the first deck where they had had experience, education, and contacts in. This was where the majority of their effort and attention was spent on. In my own case, being a senior management and technology consultant has served well as my main career.

They also had diversified in another field just in case the first one suddenly ended. This being standby careers meant tht they had a few other companies or jobs essentially waiting for them as a safety net if and when the need came up. In my case, this second-deck manifest itself as writing management books and teaching management as a visiting professor.

The third option when the first two fail to happen is to accept any job that comes around. For example, I work in Fry's Electronics getting minimum wages.

One of most admirable colleagues is Bob. His main career is being a recruiter for executives and technical people. He is great at this. He has more than thirty years of experience and he is superb in this. In addition to this, he got his certification in financial planning and he has a big set of clients whom he works with. On top of these two, he is also a certified life insurance senior salesman.

His career is a success story because he has kept being employed during the most of the global financial crisis years. Granted he did not make anywhere as much as he used to before working full time in his primary career. Yet he managed to make ends meet while so many others were unemployed.

Please note that it is not just in difficult times that the concepts described here work. The same concepts also work during the best of the financial times as well.

During those great times, using these concepts will have us get ahead faster and have better jobs. Now, having the best jobs requires that we have some margin so we can take calculated risks without losing our jobs. Most successful people are those who do take calculated risks from time to time to enrich their careers.

The important thing here is that by having the three in one career one can take some risks knowing that even if we fail, we still have some safety net in the form of the standby and desperation jobs that we can use to get back on our knees without any extended unemployment.

The interesting thing to note here is that by following the points made in this book we can have it all as far as careers are concerned. Unfortunately, on the other had unemployment makes us feel like we have lost it all.

Based on my research for many years, one thing that makes us feel that we have lost it all during unemployment is the fact that we feel that we have no control over things. We feel hopeless and not being able to control our destiny. This loss of control is what makes things difficult.

Since this book is to empower and inspire, let me say that we need to gain some control somewhere as a way of conquering the demoralizing effect of unemployment by doing what we can control.

To have it all, we need to have control over our careers and our lives by planning, setting goals and visions, and executing on them.

In a recent BBC interview with people where taken as hostages and kept under the most difficult and dehumanizing conditions, most hostages had found a way of coping by being in control of whatever they could. Most of them found being in control of their minds was would help them cope with days of torture.

We can help putting ourselves in control by refining our career skill sets by taking a class or two in one of our fine community colleges.

For example, I took one class in Foothill College that served me for many years by giving me some control as well as help me be ahead of others.

APPENDIX L
It seemed Just Like yesterday and
Barclay Simpson's Nine Principles of Business

As part of writing this book, I went back to some of the notes I'd taken while writing *Layoffs and Hope*. Scribbled on the back of a paper placemat were extensive notes I had taken talking to a good friend who'd worked for a California highways-related department for many years. We had become trusted friends during those four hour daily commutes.

I had told him that as a senior management and technology consultant I was making close to $100/Hr and he was happy for me. However, one day, totally by accident, he told me that he was getting paid $56,800/Year. I felt ashamed that I was getting three to four times more than he, granted that my consulting job required that I had to work extremely hard and that I had by far a more demanding job than he did. However, he seemed to be very content.

One particularly cold and breezy day while we were waiting for BART trains to take us to Oakland, I told him about how unhappy I was in my job.

"Bruce, I work for the public sector and you for private; I work for a first-level manager who is determined to keep me productive and happy, and your boss is some hotshot executive. Nevertheless, each day of the last forty-two years, 'It seemed just like yesterday.'"

We could not finish our conversation and I was curious to find out what that yesterday that he was talking about was. So, I called him and invited him to lunch.

"Please, please tell me what was the 'yesterday' you were talking about?" was the first thing I asked him when we were sitting down for lunch.

"Simple!" he said. Yesterday was when I had my entire family see us off from a dusty airport in South America. We almost did not make the flight since the authorities were demanding some outrageous bribe before they would let us board our flight. Finally, my cousin rolled a $50 bill and hid it in his fist and went to shake hands with the commander. During that handshake, he managed to leave that $50 bill in his hand. We were soon ordered to board our flight!

When we first arrived in America, and during the first few

years my wife and I struggled. Money was a big problem. However, worse than that was the English language that appeared like an insurmountable barrier. Each day, my wife and I would almost give up trying, and each day, we decide to give everything one last try!

"You see, America is the land of law. America gives you opportunities regardless of who you are. America is about equality!" He said as sincerely as he could, to make sure that I understood where he was coming from.

He went on to say that he still visits his country of origin as a proud American with his shiny American passport. He still loves his "old country" was one more thing he had to add.

"Well, you're a father yourself. Let me give you a friendly warning. These kids grow up much too fast. I remember when my daughter was only three years old and we would go to Capistrano, near Carmel to catch butterflies. Now she's become a dentist and has her own family." Then he admitted that no promotion or stock option would have ever made it important for him to miss those butterfly hunts!

While it is true that I learned management from Hewlett-Packard "HP Way" school of management, it is also equally true that I was lucky to be introduced to Barclay Simpson's nine principles of business. Barclay, or Barc as he is affectionately known among his employees and colleagues, is the founder of Simpson Strong- Tie.

In fact when I was working at Simpson Strong- Tie as a senior management and technology consultant my office was right across the hallway from his office.

The following article is copied from UC Berkeley News Center:

Barclay Simpson honored with Berkeley Medal

By Public Affairs, UC Berkeley | January 10, 2013

BERKELEY —

Berkeley alumnus, businessman and philanthropist Barclay Simpson has been awarded the Berkeley Medal, the university's top honor.

Simpson received the medal from Chancellor Robert Birgeneau in a small ceremony at the future site of the Berkeley Art Museum and Pacific Film Archive in Berkeley's downtown arts district shortly before the winter break. BAM/PFA director Lawrence Rinder presented Simpson with a unique memento, a brick recovered from the building site and imprinted in appreciation for Simpson's leadership in the new building project.

Alumnus Barclay Simpson after receiving the Berkeley Medal for his "positive effect on the lives around him." (Peg Skorpinski photo)

181

Birgeneau commended Simpson for his support of the BAM/PFA building campaign as well as Cal Athletics, scholarships for Berkeley students, and for campus-community programs including the Young Musicians Program, the Young Entrepreneurs at Haas and the Ailey Camp held every summer by Cal Performances.

Simpson, the founder of Pleasanton-based Simpson Manufacturing, is a member of the BAM/PFA board of directors and has served as its president and chair. He is an ardent advocate for the arts on campus and elsewhere. He and his wife, Sharon, owned a fine-arts gallery in Lafayette.

Simpson has been a major force in the initiative to replace BAM/PFA's seismically challenged museum building on Bancroft Way, and was the focus of a special tribute at the museum last May.

"In everything he does, Barc has a positive effect on the lives around him," the chancellor said in presenting Simpson with the Berkeley Medal.

The award goes to individuals whose work or contributions to society illustrate Berkeley ideals and contribute to the university's goals, and whose careers have benefited the public in exceptional ways.

Simpson said he was totally surprised by the award because he had never heard of it, and because it came at an event for BAM/PFA.

"Later I found out how important this medal was," Simpson said by phone this week. "I actually felt a little guilty. I really didn't think that I deserved it." But after learning how special the Berkeley Medal is, "it was really exciting," he added.

In the community, Simpson has supported Girls Inc. in Oakland and has served on the board of the Bay Area Rapid Transit district.

While a Berkeley student during World War II, Simpson signed up as a U.S. Naval Air Corps pilot and deployed with his fellow "Flying Golden Bears" to the Pacific following the bombing of Pearl Harbor. After an extended break from Berkeley, Simpson returned and earned a B.S. degree in 1966.

In presenting Simpson with the Berkeley Medal, Birgeneau cited the Simpson company's inspirational motto: "We learn. We grow. We put something back."

Barc is internationally known and admired for his nine principles of business which are:
1. The focus, the obsession, is on customers and users.
2. The view is long range; people never sacrifice tomorrow for the sake of today.
3. The company makes quality products that contribute to the quality of life in a significant way.
4. The company is the leader in its core business.
5. The company dignifies the contribution of every individual at every level.
6. People are excited about their jobs and the possibility for growth.
7. Innovation and creativity are encouraged; success is seldom achieved without taking risks.
8. The company feels an obligation to the system and the country that spawned it, as well as to humanity in general.
9. The company is demanding but fun place to work, where people take their responsibilities, but not themselves, seriously.

His first principle puts the emphasis on the customer as it rightly belongs to. So many companies forget that the most important thing is the customer as far as making a company success or failure. Of course, in addition to customer, employees are also as important.

So many companies get so absorbed in making a short-term profit that they forget about the customer. This actually causes them to lose market shares and makes a big dint into sales, revenue, and profits.

The second principle puts importance on the long-term nature of business. This is sharp contrast with present view from companies that are encouraged to only look at the next sixty days and make that as profitable as possible and do this at any price.

In my first book, *Layoffs and Hope*, I take the position that layoffs might seem to save some money in the short term for the company. However, in the long term the cost in loss of employee morale and mutual trust is too expensive that usually layoffs do not provide any savings.

If you carefully read the third principle you can see that quality is very important. Barc points that the products made by a company must have high level of quality and they have to contribute to the quality of life.

One of the reasons Simpson Strong- Tie has been successful is because they have established an unusually high level of product quality in safety and innovation. Before I accepted my consulting contract with them, I did some research of my own. I went to a hardware store near where I lived and asked the saleswoman about Simpson Strong-Tie. "They make great quality and they have been in business upwards of 50 years. I have been selling their products for many, many years and I have yet to hear something bad about their product.

As you can see, long-term attitude and attention to quality can make a company very successful.

The forth principle is a well known fact of business. This fact says that companies have to stick to what they can and know to do the best. Management consultants call this Centers of Excellence.

This same principle also stands true not only for our companies but also for our personal life. My friend of many years Charley loves to work as a scientist. He had struggled for years to get hired by some prestigious research company or the other. His career center of excellence is being a top notch engineer who is good in taking an already established concept or idea and to make it better. He is able in incrementally refining products. However, he has never invented or discovered anything on his own. Yet he has wasted many years trying to get a research job.

His fifth principle is very dear to my heart. He says, "The Company dignifies the contribution of every individual at every level." This is essential if you want your workers to be top notch producers and loyal to your company.

HP school of management practiced the same idea. Everybody was important and every idea was to be respected.

The sixth principle talks about work place excitement. Many top notch managers are capable of doing this well. Having mutual trust and loyalty does cultivate this contagious excitement.

The seventh principle ties creativity to success. However, it does point out the real fact that to be successful, one has to take calculated risks and even sometimes make mistakes. This is a widely accepted concept among many managers that to be a leader or a manager one can not be adverse to risk taking. Someday I would like to publish a paper that says "It is OK to make a mistake in your way to eventual success." So many people are so afraid of making mistakes that they do not take that first step. And, if one does not take that first step, there is never a chance for a successful journey.

Some of you might remember old smoke stack companies; these were companies that would pollute the air so bad that an entire city would suffer because of it. The eighth principle tells us that a company has to be good to the city and community that it is based in.

Finally, the last principle says: "The Company is demanding but fun place to work, where people take their responsibilities, but not themselves, seriously." This principle is very important in Simpson Strong-Tie work place. For example, everybody is referred to by the first name and this creates a measure of equality for all.

I saw this practice of informal equality in an Israeli company during my first visit to Tel Aviv. This contributed too much easier cooperation among people.

Come to think of it, I saw the same at HP. During a visit to HP Division that made test instruments in Colorado Springs, Colorado in the middle of winter my car got stuck in ice and mud. Colorado Springs is situated in more that 6,000 feet altitude and it has cold and windy winters.

In that cold and frosty day, I found myself in my rented car with all windows fogged and not being able to move an inch forward or backward. As I was sitting in my car completely desponded, I heard a gentle knock on the window. As I rolled down the window I noticed an older man offering to help push my car out of the ice and mud. One big push from him and my car was moving. I extended my hand for handshake. He quickly took off his gloves that had been muddied as a result of his push. "My name is Bruce Razban and I am from California. And, I am very sorry to have caused trouble for you." He said his first name and told me that it was no problem for him to push my car. I thanked him again and went our ways. At that point he looked just like any other engineer who worked at HP.

The next day, we were to work with C-Level executives at that HP division. Much to my surprise, the guy who had pushed my car was one the highest ranked individual at that HP branch.

It is needless to say that we worked extremely well together, and for many years to come.

In many of management classes, I tell graduating MBAs that a good manager must have a sense of humor or else this job can be very difficult.

Barc has truly understood this well as he points out that one has to have fun in the work place.

APPENDIX M
Dollar Amount Value of Work-Life-Balance Happiness!

According to 60 Minutes, most Americans tend to be workaholics. Most Americans think that they, too, have to make it rich quick. TV and radio news makes sure to tell us about the man or woman who did not have anything and hard work made him/her a multimillionaire.

I do know, personally, some of those who did make millions of dollars, and in a short period of time. Unfortunately, most of them are not happy. It's true that they live a great life of luxury and do not need to worry about money like the rest of us. However, to achieve that extremely high level of success, they had had to live a sickly unbalanced work life, where fourteen or eighteen-hour days were the norm.

At least in Silicon Valley, most of these success stories revolve around people who worked extremely hard and sacrificed everything. It's extremely important to keep in mind that dumb luck had to play a role in most of these ultra-successful cases.

The modern day isolation is one of the byproducts of work place toxicity and rampant and frequent layoffs.

However, imagine a full-filling job that supports American family. My Indian students have been telling me several times back in India family means parents and kids just like in America. However in India grandmothers and grandfathers and other extended family member are almost always around.

By being the CEOs of our lives and jobs, we do have a better chance of balancing the very delicate life-work balance.

Of course being CEO of your life and career requires a solid education and experience. It used to be that you would attend a university for four or more years, graduate and find a job in a career that was for a life time. These days, you need to have marketable, certifiable skill set that can be obtained from career universities. In fact successful people in life and careers have learned that education is a life-long process and that they have to take many just-in-times training to stay competitive in this difficult market. As a visiting professor, I saw Air Force Generals, former CEOs, Directors, university Deans and other attending my classes in leadership and organization development. They all had realized that to enhance their careers as well as lives, they needed to go back to these career universities from time to time to refresh their skill sets. Many of my students have told me that they regularly take time to make three or so networking calls each week just to understand who is hiring and more importantly stay in contact with friends and colleagues from the past.

The fact of the matter is that even when we have a great job, we still need to keep our eyes open and be in what is now called "perpetual job search" so as not to be caught with the dilemma of sudden job loss as it is so common these days.

In business we like to attach a dollar amount to almost everything. For example attorneys come up with a dollar amount to compensate the victim of an accident. A more modern name for this is "monetization" as it is used by the younger generation managers in the computer and Internet age.

I know a woman executive in the high-tech industry who is extremely successful and powerful. Early on in her career, she established herself as a hard-working and super intelligent person who was constantly learning new things. When I say hardworking woman I mean that she worked at least 60 hours each week and she usually had something that work related planned for the weekend too.

She and I became directors almost at the same time when she was working at IBM and I was working at Zilog. About 27 years later, we were both invited to the same management conference.

Seeing each other's name in the conference attendee list, I called her and managed to get her to arrive at the same time as I did. As we were taking about the good old times, I little girl who looked like she was about six happened to paly near us. I saw the excitement and delight in my colleague's eyes. She quickly started a conversation with the kid. Soon after that I noticed that my colleague was completely absorbed in trying to talk to this child in a language that the kid knew and play with her.

My colleague was hard at play with the kid as well as her mother for quite some time. "Bruce, I am so sad that my career took first priority day and night and it left no place for a family until it was just too late. Now I give anything to have a child. But now I am too old. My attempts to adopt and orphan has been unsuccessful and I would have loved to have had a child. I guess it will never happen!"

So, my advice, based on more than thirty years of experience is to enjoy life and your work accomplishments. Create your own incorporation libration so you will not go without a job during the down times. Being gainfully employed does require that you have your triple-decker career bus with a full tank of gas and ready with the engine running at all times.

Of course, if it turns out that you're lucky and make it very rich very quickly, then that will be fine too!

1. Using questions and exercises posed in this book, decide how the triple-decker career bus should look for you.
2. Decide what are the specific areas of expertise that are certifiable and marketable for you?
3. Study how important small businesses are, and how they can be managed well. There are several examples.
4. Study Original Joe's as a case study.
5. Call in experts in forming an incorporation or LLC, such as LegalZoom, and write down what you need to do for the incorporation libration for yourself.
6. Congratulations, once you've incorporated, you are the CEO of your company and your life. This can very well be in keeping your present job.
7. In general, you need to keep your present, or some sort of day job, until you are established in your own company.
8. Most important, find that first customer!
9. Offer that first customer to do your thing, i.e. the product or service that your company provides for free the first time. Tell them, and mean it, that there are no strings attached.
10. Once you're done, or beforehand, ask to get a letter of intent that will specify terms of payment for the second and subsequent work.
11. Offer complete satisfaction! Remember, you are the boss and you can say and mean this, and it will make your company a big success!
12. As a CEO, you are the ambassador and sales

person of your company at all times. Always act as if the next person you bump into in the hallway, bus stop, or restaurant is your next customer.

13. Do viral and Internet marketing!

14. Now, Sir or Madam CEO, you are in charge of the small business as the owner, chief, and everything. Now the sky is the limit!

Once www.jobsjobsjobsjobs.org becomes operational (around early October of 2011), we will be there for you!

One of Intel co-founders had said that "If you cannot measure it, then you cannot fix it!" Intel Corporation is of course the biggest computer chip maker in the world!

The 1% refers to the percentage of the population who has as much wealth as the other 99% combined have. This is a serious flash point, especially recently since many people are being devastated by the Global Financial Crisis. The main culprit for this is the double digit unemployment.

The 4% is the revered figure in the old American Capitalism that referred to ideal unemployment. In other words, the old system firmly believed that no matter how good the economy was, the unemployment could not be better than the 4%. This school of thought that was and is heavily ingrained in the government statistics, says that at any given time there are people in between jobs, or just not interested in working for a while. For example, those who are relocating or those who stopped working some place and got a new job somewhere else which had a starting date of a month or two off. It also included women in maternity leave, etc. Luckily today many companies respect that a father can also take some time off to help in taking care of babies.

The 99%, simply put are all of us! Out combined wealth amounts to what the 1% rich have! Fair or unfair, accurate or inaccurate this means that the top 1% has gotten rich at the expense of us the 99%!

The 107.8% was for the first time discussed in *Layoffs and Hope*. The concept is that not only the 4% is not the so called ideal best case unemployment, but it also causes a $2.4 Trillion total loss each year to our country. Furthermore, if we manage our economy and business well, we can have as much as 107.8% employment. We can achievement this 107.8% if we use:

- Good management, as in Google's, Twitter, or Facebook, etc.
- Instead of short-term present Wall Street destructive profit making, we implement the new reinvented Capitalism that uses proactive, profitable, philanthropic processes and practices.
- Following the above and applying equal emphasis on human capital as we did on materials capital, not only we will

not waste that 4% of the population, but add another 7.8% to the working population to keep them gainfully employed at all times.

Yes, I can hear you! You might be saying, "This is now Professor Razban talking!" In fact, even with my thirty years of management and technology aside, I can assure you that this is quite practical. Silicon Valley alone has achieved 0% and 1% unemployment several times. It is also important to note that Silicon Valley, by properly and legally using the H1B Visa during the height of the dot-com era had managed to import more that 10% high-tech workers from India, China, and other countries who were well received and welcome by all.

Unfortunately, since good management practices were not being used, soon there was a downturn and devastating high unemployment. The story goes that many of the new immigrants who were lured by the promise of high paying jobs to Silicon Valley were never told about the massive and frequent layoffs. Confronted with the same high unemployment, many left their rented or even purchased cars in the San Francisco Airport parking lot prior to boarding their flight back home.

Appendix P:
Laid Off Banker Liberates Himself by Selling Frankfurters

In an interesting interview in NPR Business program, an Ex banker who used to make mid to high six figures was interviewed. "As a banker, I used to make a high income and I was considered as one of the best employees. There were no indications that I will lose my job.

Did you know that Elvis Presley used to be a truck driver who actually found his passion of singing later in life?

Did you know that Tina Turner, the outstanding singer survived an abusive marriage; reinvented herself and the rest is now history.

Did you know that Dell Computers was founded by a college student who never finished college? Michael Dell, the founder and CEO of Dell has been proudly and openly talking about this from the beginning.

Each of the above had found their passion and went for it. While there is no guarantee that we will not become a second Elvis, the fact remains that trying to live the life that gives us highest job satisfaction should be what we owe to ourselves. We must give this at least one chance.

Before we go to print with this book, we decided to do one last, final, sanity check on our findings, research, and conclusions. I had run on empty for far too long; my partners who had invested more than $48,000 in this startup by personally lending me the money, working without pay, and even using their own equipment were getting somewhat impatient. With less than a quarter of gas in the tank and having no Internet at home, I had to totally rely on Libraries, Starbucks, Peet's Coffee, Denney's, and McDonald's to do my editing and writing of the book and sending it all around the world for the cover design, editing, and review.

Several times, I had to call Ed and ask him to do his ATM imitation. This typically meant that he would bring me $40 to $100 cash so I will not get stock. In one case, I had to call him from a gas station and say that I was stock; I needed him to bring money so I can put gas in my car and return home. My kid brother had lent me more than $14,000 this year alone including the time that he had to run to bank to make a cash deposit which was a credit card withdrawal that would cost him 21% interest. My therapist had not charged a penny all during the time that I was unemployed.

My wife's doctor had given her the diabetes medicine from samples that she had.

I was ready to call it quits! I was horrified about winning, and I was horrified about losing. I could not take either of the two consequences, so it seemed like it was time to quit.

I had promised my friends to do the one last research to make sure that we have not collectively gone crazy with the content of this book. They say that the teacher appears when the student is ready. This is exactly what happened to put a teacher in front me when I badly needed him.

I had seen the gas gauge keep going down showing me I had less and less gas to drive around to find a parking place in the Palo Alto Library to finish this book that day. But, as I was entering the library, somebody was calling my name from behind. This was the voice of my old friend. I sat down with him to talk about the good old days. I told him that I had just been given a visiting professor job at a university and that I was also seriously thinking about semi-retirement and living on that income. While all of this was boring to both of us, then I decided to tell him that I had just submitted the final manuscript to my dear friend Walter who is a Pulitzer Prize nominee and hope to have the book published soon. However, we think that I must find one last person to interview to make sure the book is OK. It seemed like we both were getting excited. "Bruce, you do not say! You wrote a book? Man I am impressed! This is fantastic! Good for you!" was his reaction. I proudly had to correct him that this will be my fourth published book!" His voice going up one octave, "Bruce, you did what? You did four books and not just one? How could this be?"

I told him that in spite all this effort, I only had a few weeks until my house would be auctioned in a foreclosure sale. I could see that he really was sympathetic. I told him that I was set to do a book signing event at Kepler's Bookstore in Menlo Park but I lacked the $150 to buy the books to take there. Usually writers make some money buying their own book at wholesale price and then selling them at full value during readings or book reviews.

To my pleasant surprise, he gave me three $50 bills. "Bruce, do not lose your chance. You will feel a lot better when you tell people about your artistic and scholarly work of writing books!" He asked me how I was doing financially. I told him that I had to go without a job for more than two years and my writing was the only way that I could keep my sanity. "Bruce, please, please, please, please come to my store! I have fresh Jewish bread Calah that I have just baked for the Jewish New Year! Please come! Do it for me." Then just to make sure, he asked, "Is two O'clock good?"

The hopelessness resulting from lack of a job and intensive effort to publish the fourth book had already taken their tolls on me. I was tired and not generally in good mood. I twice decided to call him and apologize for not being able to go there as promised. However, I could not let him down and I try to be a man of my words. His store is in one of the best streets in Palo Alto near Stanford University. For more than a decade we had been going there for great bagels, hallahs, and other Jewish food. His place is Kosher. This means that food has to be prepared with strict standards in health and cleanliness. Furthermore, all of this has to be under the watchful eyes of a Rabbi.

I asked him if he was willing to be interviewed since I was publishing a book about economy and especially unemployment. "Sure!" This was his answers with excitement. By then we had done the interview so many times that we knew exactly how long it took and what were the most typical answers. So, I all I had to do was to make sure the certain things were true. I asked him if he was the owner/CEO of Authentic Flavor Ezzi's Brooklyn Bagels! He said yes and I am proud of it. The he added that he had a BS degree from NYU and that he had worked at some company for about a year before he decided to take matters in his own hand and start doing what he really wanted to do. After a few false starts, he decided that he wanted to make a bakery.

He did seem to be that CEO of his career and life that I had defined in my book. I could clearly see that he had complete mutual trust and loyalty between him, employees, and customers. Many customers were repeat customers who came there for years and years and they all knew him. The ambient was warm and the establishment was clean. The food was of high quality, and he was constantly interested in making it even better. He would cordially ask customers as they came about how happy they were with him and his breads. Also, to my astonishing surprise, he knew the names of customers' spouses, and children as well.

"Mr. Razban, for a while I had great competition. A franchised bagel shop of even good reputation started a branch just one block away from me. In some cases their prices were even lower than I could possibly produce. They also had massive advertising. We had to close shop for nine days. We just thought that we could not compete." Then he went on to say, "Each day I would get tons of calls. My customers were assuring me that they will continue to buy from me since they have been happy with me for many years; they would not let the price bother them; they loved that authentic taste, service, and experience that only my store could offer them. One customer told me that my competition was awesome, but I was more awesome than they could ever be."

"I had to reopen my store. The word got around, and each day there would be a line of customers trying to buy and even hoard my bagels!" He said while he was drinking a cup of coffee. I asked him what made him happy with being his own boss. "Bruce it is the freedom; the freedom to feel being needed; freedom to be there for the customer; freedom to make sure that you and your entire team adds value." This was his most straightforward answer. Then he could not wait to add, "I wish major corporations learned to do the same for their customers as well!" I noticed that he had lowered his voice to tell me something very confidential. He said, "Bruce, I had an employee who got sick and ended up losing almost all his savings. We all pitched in and made sure that he had more hours if we wanted and we made sure that we would cover for him when had to go to those frequent doctor appointments. Just seeing that he is healthy and he cares for his team and customers, is worth every penny of additional cost that we as a team had to pay to help him out!" I asked him about layoffs. He most confidently said, "I will do everything possible to avoid it. I try to find out what is causing us to lose business; I will try to help my employees provide even better service; I will let them work less hours while I work more to make sure we do not lose customers." Then, I asked him about firing. "Again, Bruce, you want to do everything to hire good employees and then you have to take care of them as if you are their relative. Then 90% of time, even the worst employees improve and improve and in some cases they become your best employees!"

Unknown to him, he was telling me exact same words that I had heard from Sir Richard Branson regarding his Virgin Atlantic Airline. These same principles that work for a small bakery, also works for a big corporation.

Therefore, I like to recommend Authentic Flavor Ezzi's Brooklyn Bagels in Palo Alto as my second show case. My other showcases are HP of the fifties, sixties, and seventies; National

Semiconductor Corporation as it was transformed and lead by Dr. Gil Amelio; and Plantronics. Of course, these are based on my own firsthand experience. You might take issue with some of the big names here, but please note that companies, big and/or small take the shape that their management gives them at some specific period of time and experience in one group can be much better or worse than another. This is so because no less than 70% of employee job satisfaction comes from the immediate manager.

I had for years admired this friend for his excellent management and interpersonal skills. He is a patient, nice, and mellow man who genuinely cares for others. He was telling me the almost exact things that I had heard from my previous showcase, the Original Joe's manager in San Jose. They both were genuinely interested in treating customer and employee right. They both had found their own "thrill" and they both had learned that the name of the game is service to the customer. Neither one seemed to be that impressed with any advertising except for the word of mouth. This means one happy customer telling another and another and it does pile up.

"Bruce, it took a lot of guts for me to start this business! However, it has paid off! Of course, it was good for me to work for a year or two in some company to learn the ropes before I started my own business." However, being our own CEO and the freedom that it provides is worth all the risk.

Remember what I was told from a recent immigrant: "I agree that lots things are not that great in the US today. But, this is still the land of law, and opportunity. However the most important thing is the freedom." This last part of the sentence echoed Honorable George Shultz, the former Secretary of State's word, "Bruce, this is a free country! You can say and do whatever you want!"

Ageism Rageism!

Written by: Bruce Razban

Article Overview: As an entrepreneur, and an established Senior Management and Technology Consultant, and against my own advice, I tried to test the waters once more and find a job. I was quickly and bitterly reminded of the dire consequences of working for others!

Ageism Rageism!

Having gone almost one year without any paychecks or consulting assignments, and being rejected repeatedly with excuses such as being "Overqualified", or "Not a Good Fit", or "Professionally Obsolete", I decided to do something about this.

After all, one of my colleagues had quickly dropped thirty-five or more pounds, colored her blonde and gray hair black, and gotten a facelift operation on borrowed money just to get a job. In fact she also had to re-learn how to giggle, just to hide her actual age. She carefully described the painful steps she had gone through to "chop off" years from her age, and to appropriately act dumb proportionally to hide her superb experience that companies used to pay a mint to hire. "Never say in the old days, we did this work this way", she cautioned me. "Never mention anything about older technology" she mentioned in passing. Then as if she had remember a national security secret she raised her voice a bit and said, "Never", with a big pause combined with deep remorse. "Never, answer the question about your favorite TV show that may indicate your age!" "I know!", then after a deep breath and a big pause, she continued that "A recruiter tricked me with this question and guessed my actual age."

I heard about another colleague that shaved his head to get rid of "Discrimination Grays" and started to wear colorful shirts with colored T-shirts that showed when he did not completely buttoned his shirts to hide the fact that like me he is around sixty years old too. The fact that he had a patent grant had to be hidden too since that would clearly self criminate him and deluge his "Advanced" age! He could only list one of his published books for the same reason.

What a travesty!

According Richard Bolles the famous author of "What Color is Your Parachute?" books, at this age people are to use all that valuable experience they had and create masterpieces. The analogy he used in his book was that, just like an opera, this advanced age is when we create arias in concerts. Arias that are the peak, the optimal that experience can produce. Richard Bolles is internationally known as the authority in career development and management. "Mr. B." as he is affectionately known among his followers of many years, including me, knows what he is talking about.

Against my own best judgment that I should use my gold experience as a Senior Management and Technology Consultant and continue my own entrepreneurship consulting practice, I decided to mimic my colleagues, and "Age Sanitized" my resume to just show "Recent Experience", and removed graduation dates. I offered to work as a volunteer for no money in a PHP professional membership group in San Francisco. I got several takers. It was for free after all!

One well funded startup in downtown Palo Alto, CA enthusiastically invited me to meet with them. When the CEO who is less than half my age saw me, could not hide his surprise, disappointment, and disbelief. Yet, he tried to go through the motions as best he could. We started with some small talk about American Idol TV show. I had taken my colleague's advice to heart. Then, we moved to his questions. But, after thirty years of experience, I could easily see his struggle to find right words to politely and yet not abruptly terminate this awful waste of time.

He disappointedly finally concluded that I "Look OK" to him, but he had to get "Permission of his CTO". He even bothered to ask for my availability for the next week. We shook hands, and he hurriedly walked me through the several cubicles occupied by employees who seemed to be at most twenty-five. One of them pretended that he had not even noticed this "Old Token" passing by, and the other did a half hand gesture of sort of waving.

The verdict came in a week later after the CTO decided not to even meet with me.

I was "Overqualified, and, Not a Good Fit." This came as a double rejection! I guess they were telling me that ageism has created such rageism that I was unacceptably overpriced even for free!

Abject Executive Poverty

Written by: <u>Bruce Razban</u>

Article Overview: If you, as an executive are not happy, then you might want to read my story of round trip rags to riches. I, as an executive, was not happy either with all that "stuff" that money could buy. There was an emptiness that expensive suits, business class travel, and four or five star hotels could not fill. Yet, as an aftermath of Global Financial Crisis that cost my tiny company $180,000, I realized what real happiness was all about.

Abject Executive Poverty

There was a time when I had become a director of a major corporation at a relatively young age. I was proud and excited about my promotion. I was in charge of a multi-million dollar budget for the first time and almost seventy people in my group.

I felt that justice had finally been done and I was rewarded what I had worked for so hard for many years. I was a popular manager and I got along with just about anyone. However, the most important thing was that I produced fantastic products and services for my company. I was considered the best of the best! I made the seemingly impossible engineering task to happen. Furthermore, thanks to my ceaseless desire to learn and study, I had mastered the art and the science of team building. Almost in all projects we produced heroics, while team member were learning new things and had fun doing what was their task.

As opposed to my first trips to Europe while I was a student and on a student budget requiring that I sleep in trains on overnight travel to save money, I now would fly business class and stay in four star hotels.

I had been the quintessential American story of going from rags to riches. I had arrived in California on a Greyhound bus with the $300 that I had borrowed from my best friend. Now, I was a director!

Nevertheless, I had never forgotten my humble origins. I still loved and enjoyed the good and rich life, but, I felt that I owed to others to help them as a way of saying thanks.

I was one of the first to buy $1,000 Nordstrom suits, and $200 Hickey-Freeman shirts. In addition I would buy suits and shirts from a catalogue house in Hong Kong. Each suit would be tailor made based on 30 or more measurements.

All that "stuff" meant success to me! I had escaped the abject poverty of college years and earlier career. I never had to balance my checkbook as there always was enough money. There even was money to play. I never had to worry about the next meal of the next car payment or anything.

I paid cash for my Lexus and drove it on picturesque California Highway 1 along the Pacific coast.

As my salary kept going up and I was trying to become a Vice President and then the CEO of a major corporation, I started to feel emptiness combined with guilt that not everyone had succeeded as much as I had. As my frequent flyer mileage card with United Airlines became a Platinum card, I realized that I had more miles that I could use. So, I gave away some to friends and family. I sent them free tickets. Some were able to have vacations that they had never had and would never have had if it was not for my gift.

However, inside that shell there still was the man that I had been in college with faded blue jeans and severely limited budgets for anything including essentials of life. A movie or concert was a major event and I would be elated by some non-important things as a day trip to Chicago on a Greyhound bus.

Then the Global Financial Crisis hit!

This time being CEO of a tiny consulting company, I was hit and was hit really bad. Fear of foreclosure, inability to pay bills not just for the company, but myself started to create unbelievable stress. I was not alone. Many of my friends had been hit just as bad too.

After about 18 months, one day, I noticed that I had accepted a contract for less than $300 and I was really grinding to make sure I made the deadline. Working day and night, I finally made it. As I was treating myself to a McDonald steaming cup of coffee, I noticed that my faded blue jean just looked like those I would wear in college.

It seemed that I had a round trip rag to riches and back to rags again. "What this cannot be! I worked 32 years and wrote a management book, to be back to where I had started as a typical and poor college student. Wow! How could this be?" I repeatedly asked myself.

Enjoying that steaming cup of coffee and being one among those who were not executives somehow made me feel at home. This was real! Those fancy hotels and business class travel were not.

"But 18 months without a contract has brought you to abject poverty! Look at yourself! Look at your Lexus which is in dire need of new tires! You, former executive, are living below the International Poverty Line now!" This echoed in my mind. This was pounding on a mind that was poisoned with self shame and blame for having lost close to $180,000.

Suddenly, an interesting revelation seemed to clear the air. There was clean and clear air that can be inhaled after a big thunderstorm.

So long as you took these 18 months to help others who were trying to find jobs, so long as you wrote an uplifting book to those who had lost their jobs, what you have now with this worn out blue jeans is not abject poverty.

"The abject poverty in your case was when you were rich and when you attempted to forget or cover up your humble beginnings. You tried, but luckily that emptiness and guilt prevented you to forget about all those who were less fortunate than you were!" This was playing in mind over and over again.

That was the abject executive poverty!

"You are now filthy rich! Remember the family friend who came to the train station to buy you train ticket to go for your interview? Remember the best friend who lent you $12,000 so you will not lose your house? Remember the other friend who interrupted his lunch to come and give a lift when you did not have cash to even take a bus?" This was my happy and satisfying self talk!

I was indeed filthy rich, even though not in dollars!

Appendix S:
Beware of Unemployment, Underemployment, Unhappy Employment Spillover to Relationships and Life

To the best of my humanly best, I have made this book inspiring, uplifting, informative, as well as empowering. Many people who had read the first, second, and third manuscripts had told me that book was effective in helping them understand and act proactively in not only the job search but also in career management.

Then one day a student told me that "Soon after I had lost my job in an unfair and unexpected layoff, my wife of fifteen years decided to file for divorce!" After going silent for a few moments, he added, "Our marriage had been OK until that darn layoff. However, somehow after that we started to fight more and more over money and seemingly unimportant things! I could not take the rejections in the work place as well as having a demoralizing battlefield at home." Then pointing to a chapter in the textbook, he wanted to know what my experience has been with this.

While it was true that I was his professor and teaching a management course that graduating MBA students were taking, I was only half qualified to answer his question. I had the answer from management; however, I was not a marriage counselor. Assuring that these things happen, I shared my thirty years of experience with him. My experience seemed to tell me to advise him to try to diffuse the situation and try to somehow buy some more time while looking for a job as well as the ordeal of job search.

Of course, this gets worse when children are concerned. As fathers and mothers, I know that some of us will give everything we have to just provide for them. Then, when there is no job and/or no money things get worse and worse.

One of the best strategies I have seen to cope, survive, and even thrive in these situations is what an old colleague did.

He decided that:

- Even though he was unemployed, he had a full time job of finding a new job or several part-time jobs.
- He decided to be a full time job seeker from 8:00 AM to 5:00 PM and then the rest of the day being primarily a parent.
- He was smart enough to quickly realize that he needed

help. One telephone call to his church resulted in several different avenues of help offered to him.

- Also, luckily he quickly softened his wife's heart by agreeing to see a marriage consular that both approved for help.

I saw him a few months later in a professional conference. With a broad smile he told me that his wife has decided not to go through with the divorce for the time being since things were improving.

Interestingly enough, my colleague was still unemployed, yet he seemed to be much happier than before.

Appendix T:
It was Mismanagement that got us into Global Financial Crisis; it is Management that will get us Out of it

"Professor Razban, I have had enough of talking heads talking empty talk of statistics on TV. I also do not think that governments can solve this Global Financial Crisis on their own!" This was what a senior engineer shared with me. He had gone without a job for more than two years and he had decided to get an MBA so as to have a better chance competing in the job market. Evidenced by how global the unemployment problem is, it proves the point that a new management technology needs to be used to overcome it. In many people's opinion, the entire Global Financial Crisis was created by mismanagement. As such, it is proper management that will solve the problem.

As Dr. Elizabeth Kubbler-Ross has found, coping with this crisis will start anger and denial. People will get angry at each other; also some people totally deny that a crisis exists. "Depending on who you listen to, it is always the other bastards that have caused this problem; there is a conspiracy; it is us against them and them against us; it is always with the promise that things will get better." Was another observation that my star student came up with.

As late as November of 2012, in a BBC World Debate there were alarms that at best our future financial recovery will be very sluggish and we see extremely high unemployment that causes people to detach from the work force and thus become permanently unemployable.

While this is a scary prediction, there seems to be many signs of it happening. For example in Greece and other poorer European countries unemployment of above 20%, along with the street riots seem to have become nightly TV news items.

This book tries to instantly optimize your career and job prospects so that you will not be part of this sorry picture.

After thirty years of experience in this business, I have come up with the conclusion that if we do a better job of planning we will not get into these problems. We must plan, resource, and execute as any decent management book tells us we should do.

One of my mentors from HP had told me several times that it is not the problem that is important. His view was that we must understand the problem and then instead of blaming and being angry we need to use our energies in solving the problem or at least managing the problem.

The world is what it is. Things do go wrong; disasters do happen. However, we owe it to ourselves to do teamwork and solve problems.

In today's technologically advanced world, we must find ways not to waste our lives in some dead end job in a dysfunctional environment. If we manage our lives and careers better, and with the almost unlimited help from high-tech we will succeed beyond our imagination.

Remember that you are the CEO of your career, your job, and your life!

Believe me, being in charge of your career and life rather than leaving this critically important thing in the hands of others and just random chance will not give you better life. You must take charge and do it now by being your own CEO.

Let me give you a taste of how CEOs think and act. For example, Jeff Smister, CEO and Chairman of United Airlines in a Charlie Rose Show in August of 2013 was saying these things:

1. "I, as the CEO am responsible to make people's life measurably better!"
2. "I will build credibility over time."
3. "I will make the work place at United Airlines so much better that our employees would want to, and, not be told to do and deliver."
4. "The key to success is long-term stability!"
5. "What matters is the service to the customer."
6. "I will make my company dependable and reliable!"

He should know, he runs the world's biggest Airline, the United Airlines that has 5,500 flights each day across the globe.

Hw as the CEO says that he is doing these things for his company. But, these are the same things that we can do for ourselves when we accept being the CEO of our life and career and/or being the CEO of our small business that we made for ourselves.

We must choose peace, love, and success instead of hate and all the death and destruction that can be brought on us by ourselves at the speed of light.

The same super destructive force that can literally devastate our humanity as we know it, can serve us in creating health and prosperity that people will be amazed to see.

Many people in 2008 to 2011 blamed the CEOs and Board of Directors as being the culprits that brought us the agony of global financial crisis. In my opinion, these CEOs and Board of Directors are not purely at fault; it is not greed that is driving them to this; it is the fact that management as they knew it has changed and has changed drastically. As such many of these executives do not really know what to do and how to do it to manage things better.

They find themselves at a total loss when it comes to understanding and working with human and intellectual capitalism. Also, it has been my experience that many of these C-Level executives are having a serious problem dealing with the global aspect of things.

During lunch, one executive who had read my second draft of this book took me to task. "Prof. Razban, I can see a truck as an example of materials capital. What on earth are you talking about when you talk about American global capitalism?" Then he added, "With my truck, I can move that much dirt each day and make some money. What on earth are you talking about the new capitalism that takes into account human intellectual capital? I can show you a truck, but you cannot show me this so called new reinvented brand of capitalism. As if this was not enough, you go further to tell me that to make a lot of money, I have to practice proactive profitable philanthropy." A few seconds later, he decided to let me really have it. "Sir, I have to work for a living. Unlike you, I cannot deal with theories and ideas each working day. I need to go make money!"

Then he took is gold Visa card and gently yet firmly put it on the table. "See, my way works; my way is practical!"

A few weeks later, in a chance encounter, he had to get my attention by saying, "Hey I read your book after it was published. Do you really mean it that you do not have anything against CEOs making more and more money? How does that work exactly?" Then as if trying to impress me, he added, "It is people, human intellectual capital and Internet that when augmented with old materials-based capitalism that does it! Does it not?"

In a blockbuster movie called "Top Gun", a pilot gets too scared of flying again. His father's name was not something that this pilot could be proud of even though his father did the right thing while fighting for America.

This pilot whose name is Maverick, was doing outstanding things in dog fights with the enemy and everyone respected him. Unfortunately due to something that was not a fault of his own, his F14 state-of-the-art "Tomcat" suddenly went through a controllable circular and vicious downward motion resulting in a crash and burn that killed his flight partner, the navigator.

I am hoping that by now you can associate "not being our faults" to layoffs. In fact just like layoffs Maverick had also internalized this. In his mind, his buddy the copilot would have steel been alive had it not been for his mistake.

The commander, who had served in Vietnam, was doing his best to help his best pilot Maverick fly again. "Maverick, I lost four of the seven of my men in a dog fight. Dog fights are what we do up in the sky!"

Even that did not convince Maverick to stop his self-directed anger and resume flying.

However, later in the movie when the call of duty comes, Maverick shows his courage and destroys the enemy fighters.

Preparing to meet some friends visiting from Europe, I called the Hyatt Regency in the heart of San Francisco business district to find out if they have their usual lights and an amazing train set several stories high surrounded by the most beautiful ginger bread houses for the holidays. "Sir that show is no longer since the man who used to set it up passed away in 2008. The majestic Equinox revolving restaurant on the top of the hotel is also closed. Sorry, Sir, however, we still have our Christmas trees decorated!" This was the finely trained and extremely hospitable receptionist told me. "Wow, I used to work in PG&E just across the street and every Christmas I bring several guests to enjoy the elegant show. Children especially would get mesmerized with the train set. We will miss this." This was what I shared from the bottom of my heart. My guests from Israel and Japan and I went somewhere else this time.

Things are just not what they used to be! The radio in the

taxi cab was talking about a few more European countries losing their credit ranking and having to deal with sky high interest rates.

On another occasion, there was a program devoted to high school kids not being able to take this financial crisis too well. After all, kids are kids and they expect a shelter that is not foreclosed, cloths, food, and gifts. Unfortunately several of these kids had taken their own lives.

Then there was a program in KQED Radio about a charity organization which had had to let go of several workers after the massive budget cuts. Never the less, the charity organization was doing the best they could to help kids from broken and traumatized homes get the art therapy that they needed so badly.

Then there was another program about a French-born American who had donated $125 Dollars around the world for charities.

I strongly believe in the power of art and music in general to heal. Don't you?

I used to think that heroes were never scared while they were in a life and death situation in some battle field. Later on based on many university research and discussions with actual fighter pilots I discovered that they are scared too. However, the let the scared feeling come and go and then they do the best they can for that moment, minute, or more in the height of the battle.

We too need to keep improving ourselves and making sure that we do have continued and hopefully gainful employment to let these difficult times pass by!

In early 2009, I called in as I have done many times since I consider Ronn a legend with a great following. His guest that day was a lady who had just written a book about socio-economic impact of layoffs. I was warmly received and when I shared my own experience I could see that people were interested. All of his before anybody had predicted how bad things will get. He frequently has outstanding guests and we have Lexus, Blackberry, and love of gadgets in common.

Appendix V:
"General Commander" Howard Shultz of Starbucks

Howard Shultz is one of the best CEOs since he does indeed follow some of the guidelines that I have pointed out in this book. He provides a better working condition for his employees; Starbucks employees seem to enjoy a higher level of mutual trust and loyalty; in addition, Starbucks employees tend to be much more proud of their jobs and company than many other companies. During a three day holiday, I sent an email to Howard Shultz after reading a book that was written about Starbucks. In matter of hours I got a response directly from him. The email exchange continued and I even sent him several suggestions.

Then I came across a book written by an older unemployed man who had several problems. That man was finally hired by Starbucks and he was treated with the utmost respect and care. Having worked in a positive environment, helped the older gentleman to slowly get his life together and get a new lease on a happier life.

As you might know, I am Gold Medalist writer in Evan Carmichael. One of my first articles that published there two years ago is the following management article in my management coach section:

"Ice Water Test of Starbucks Strategy, Implementation, and Tactical"

A simple test sometimes verifies and validates what thousands of pages of strategy documents cannot. A simple request at a Starbucks, and the response in superior service, convinced me of the strategy excellence at Starbucks.

I have read almost all books regarding Howard Schultz, the CEO of Starbucks and the company. Reading these books as a Senior Management Consultant with 32 years of experience was helpful to me.

However, the real test of Howard's excellence at making an outstanding company, culture, community, and operation happened totally by accident. At the end of tiring day far away from home, and totally disappointed about the outcome of several meetings, I decided to go to nearest Starbucks. As I entered the store, I realized that I had left my wallet in the office. Therefore, I had no money. I called a colleague and he promised to bring my wallet in about half an hour.

While looking at the menu, I decided to ask for an Ice Water. The Baristas (staff) almost jumped to make sure they give me that perfect cup. "How much ice would you like?" "Would you like a small or big cup?" Then there was the question that they did not ask. They did not ask

"Anything else to go with this?" It was clear to me that they had already anticipated my panic for having no money with me. "Please feel free to come back for a refill, if you like. It is free!" They did seem genuinely interested in serving me.

There was absolutely no difference on how I was treated this time and other times when I would spend a lot more than others and buy many drinks and snacks. Closing time approached fast and there was no sign of my colleague bringing my valet. I noticed the person who had served me my ice water glass was politely offering me a chocolate chip cookie in a small bag. "Sir, I bought too many of these for myself. Would you like one of them?"

"How long have you worked for Starbucks?" He said "two years." "Tell me, honestly, how is it to work here?" Before he could answer, I had guessed. They must feel good about their job. This high level of job satisfaction helped them treat me so well. There must have been a great deal of mutual trust and loyalty. The employees in this Starbucks and many other places I have visited demonstrate a sense of empowerment and confidence that makes superior service almost effortless and routine for them. They do it and show it with each tiny aspect of their work. This practice is second nature to them. As these thoughts were parading on my mind, I noticed that the employee was starting to tell me his honest answer.

His answer was, "Starbucks takes good care of me, and I take good care of Starbucks and all Starbucks Customers!" Then he rushed to add, "I must say, working here is not just work. It is also fun!" He also hesitantly added that, "No place is always perfect, but this comes closest to being one."

I had sensed the same feeling of pride and confidence with the Starbucks CEO when he personally replied to my email.

That one ice water cup validated all that was written in "Pour Your Heart Into It", *It is Not About Coffee*, or "The Starbucks Experience". In addition, that ice water cup, gave me warm heart-felt meaning of Michael Gates Gill's book, *How Starbucks Saved My Life*. This book had resonated with me before since I have a lot in common with Michael.

So, Howard, Onward and Upward! Great job!

Do you think that I am too generous in my complements to Starbucks? Maybe I am and maybe not. The fact remains that a good part of this book was written in several different Starbucks branches using the Starbucks Wi-Fi network and drinking coffee to stay awake. However, the main point is that either other major corporations learn to be like Starbucks or they lose business.

Of course Starbucks is not perfect.

Having said all of these, I heard something interesting from the Santa Clara supervisor. She said, "They give me insurance benefits; they trust and respect me; when I had to take some time off to take care of some urgent matter, the other team members treated me as if I was part of the family. Now, every time a customer walks in; every time a customer wants something, I remember that Starbucks family cared for me so I care for Starbucks by caring for Starbucks customers."

On another occasion, the barrister who poured my coffee in the Menlo Park Starbucks right before you drive on to Dumbarton Bridge, told me that he takes pride in being the best he can be and working for a company that respects and empowers employees to honestly take pride in working for the best of the best.

OK! I can hear you! You are asking me to tell you something bad about Starbucks. I hear you! Here you go:

Howard Schultz appeared in a news program and looked just like other over polished CEOs parroting meaningless sound bites. In one occasion he even looked to the right as if to get the next clues from his PR gurus. Now, if I was to talk to him, I will tell him "Howard, you do not need these things; just be yourself and tell your story. You will be even more respected and liked." I would, as an executive coach recommend that maybe he would be the trusted company man who can start a meaningful dialogue with the unemployed and for the purpose of breaking the distrust that is rampant everywhere.

During the 2011 holiday season, I noticed that Starbucks had a special plan to help people find jobs. This is a case of a little proactive philanthropy helping companies use honesty and become even more popular and make more money.

Sooner or later the word will get around that if companies indeed take care of their intellectual capital, human aspects, and being customer-centric, they will win beyond any imagination.

"Sheriff of Wall Street" in Michael Krazny's KOED Forum
Program

I am a fan of more than 30 years of San Francisco Bay Area KQED radio and TV programs. I enjoy the informative and interesting programming that could only result when radio and TV programming would liberate themselves from the super commercialism that limits other stations.

In particular, I love the Forum program by Dr. Michael Krazny. Finally after all these years I got a chance to go to one of his book signing events at JCC in Los Gatos, California. However, it still remains my dream to someday be a guest on his program. Since his program is repeated at 10:00 PM night, I get a chance to listen to it while I am crossing the Dumbarton Bridge after many hours of teaching. This program invigorates my thoughts and makes the driving tolerable.

In one recent program he had Elliot Spitzer who was a former Attorney General of New York. Spitzer is also known as Sheriff of Wall Street as he really tried to clean up some of what is now known as Wall Street corruption.

I was jolted in my seat while driving my car over Dumbarton Bridge that he and I have a great deal of agreement on problems with our present economy. However, it seems that my first book, *Layoffs and Hope* had predicted things back in middle of 2008.

"Michael, the CEO compensation that used to be 40 to 1 in the sixties, where 1 is the salary of the average employee in the company, sky rocketed to 550 to 1 a few years ago and even now in the midst of the Global Financial crisis, it is still 350 to 1."

In think that Spitzer was just too kind to the CEOs. I think that he should have added that most CEOs are now not respected or liked and most Americans cannot trust them. Most importantly, most of them are perceived as incompetent. The reason what Americans think that they are incompetent is that Americans are holding CEOs responsible for the devastating job losses.

However, I, as a senior management and technology consultant will share with you that the problem is that CEOs are still trying to use that obsolete old American Capitalism and not the reinvented American Global Capitalism that manages human and intellectual capital just as much if not more than the old one.

Also the reinvented one can move at the speed of Internet and understands and integrates Social Networking and new gadgets.

Spitzer advocates for the Occupy Wall Street movement to make sure they have five top clear and crisp goals; communicate them and make sure they happen. He pointed out that one of those five points must be mortgage reform.

President Bill Clinton in his book *Back to Work* advocates co-operation between the private sector and government as necessary for restoring prosperity. Remember that during his presidency, America had as much prosperity as it ever had. In fact this book is talking about a proven thing that made Brazil so successful. The government of Brazil and its private sector decided to honestly co-operate with each other.

Another interesting thing is that already many people have decided that just one career is not enough anymore. For example in my own case, I have made a quarter-Decker career for myself. Also in the case of William Carlos William, who is the author of "So Much Depends" he refers to himself in New York Times Book Review section as doctor-poet! The hyphenation is telling us that he had more one career to be safer in the work place as well as being a multidimensional human coping with the demands of Digital Humanity.

In my opinion that program was one of the best!

Never the less, what we need now is expert management to put America back to work. Jobs were and continue to be the number one source of all our disasters now.

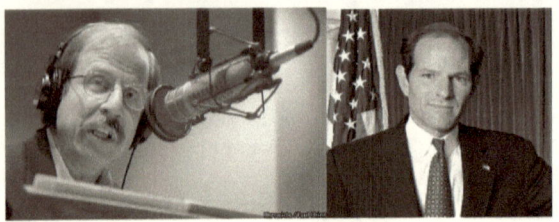

APPENDIX X
Digital Humanity, Integrity, and Code of Global Operational Ethics

In the old capitalism, CEOs and Board of Directors could make money any way they wanted and then get that money and run. When, CEO compensation was 550 to 1 compared to average employee, these things could and did happen.

Many companies took the position that they had to pay those high salaries and bonuses to keep their CEOs. However, it was the mismanagement on the side of those very CEOs that got us into this Global Financial Crisis. Never the less, companies argued that they had to do this to keep those incompetent CEOs. Unfortunately, so many of those CEOs in those companies had to just be fired for doing such a bad job.

Not only they did not get fired, they found a way to get more promotions or just go to another company and mess them up too at a higher salary.

However, as Professor Dietmeyer of Wisconsin had told us in 1960's "In this coming digital world everything and anything can either be true or false. It cannot be both."

So if a company is not "cash register" honest about their business; about the treatment of their employee human and intellectual capital they would be discovered by digital humanity at the speed of Internet.

Do you remember those smoke stack industries? They polluted the entire community in the process of producing products at any price. Now when a CEO, for example former CEO of British Petroleum (BP) causes one of the worst disasters in the business history and then goes yachting, that information goes viral in no time on Internet and would get then cost them their jobs much quicker than before.

In the new order of things then the new Global Code of ethics will be computed and recorded globally at the speed of light. Imagine if SOX regulations could be digitally executed in each and every transaction. This will force companies to be honest about their real and honest advertising, employee treatment, and value added service to customers.

This creates a global antidote to the viscous cycle created by layoffs. Consider the following:

1. High consumer satisfaction products,
2. High sales and profits, then
3. Company invests these profits into its operating material capital and human intellectual capital,
4. Better products and services used in a rule-based systematic company processes that results in higher mutual trust and loyalty producing a successful, productive work environment,
5. More profits, results in more productivity,
6. Back, successfully to Step 1 and no need for knee jerked

execution of layoffs resulting in viscous cycles and destroys economy.

Remember that everything can be either true or false at the same time.

However, instead of fixing blames on CEOs, I soon realized that a lot of them work extremely hard and a lot of them are really in trouble. This goes for most of the C-Level executives that I know as well. During a coffee break, I heard these sincere words from a CEO. "Bruce, I am a loss. What worked well in the 80s and 90s does not seem to work anymore. With my education in the 90s, I learned to do things a certain way and I was really good at that, now it seems that none of those things work anymore." His sincere words jolted me to think why things were the way they were. Why there was almost no job security? Why so many people were unemployed? And of course much more importantly, what is a solution.

This was what motivated and empowered me to write this book. I think that I have found a good and effective way to help people be the CEO of their jobs and lives as a way of minimizing the negative effects that all these layoffs, offshoring, and downsizings have done.

For years I used to have a rusted battery connection framed and hung in my living room. Please let me indulge in telling you yet another story. The story begins in a cloudy and rainy day during a particular winter in San Francisco Bay Area that had had much too much rain that year. I had to take highway 880 which is notorious for choking during rush hours and being not well designed. All of sudden my car's engine just stopped cold. I was lucky to take my nearest exit and three really nice people volunteered to push my car to the nearest gas station. "Sir, you have a serious engine problem. This will cost you a lot of money to repair. In fact at that moment I was convinced that I must have a serious problem." I used the payphone and called a friend who is really good with cars. He was there in less than fifteen minutes. In another ten minutes bending on my engine, he pulls this rusted battery connected and its wires out and laughs and says, "Bruce, you major engine problem is this rusted connector. Then he disappears in his own car and comes back with a $12 kit that had everything to repair the battery connectors." In another fifteen he was done. "I bet you a cold glass of beer that your engine will start as soon as you turn the switch!" Well the engine did and everything was fine.

This proved to me that sometimes most complex and huge problems have a simple solution. And, that is why I framed that rusty connecter and hung it on my wall. What this taught me that a seemingly $2,000 or $3,000 problems can be solved by a $12 solution.

For decades now we have been using the nStep concept of management. John Kotter, who is one of my heroes and MIT scholar in management, has put together a globally accepted 8 step solution to be used in organizational transformations. This is what we teach in our graduate MBA classes, and this is what has worked for several decades. However, this only solves ½ of the problem that has to do with tangible and practical side of management and the material based only brand of capitalism. This can and is programmed in computers and our MBA students usually have no problem understanding and applying this as it is somewhat of a simple solution.

Now, we need to complete the other ½ of this equation by using cash register honesty programmed just like SOX can be programmed in our computers and use the well known concept of rule based computing to make sure we are also taking into consideration the digital humanity and human intellectual capital and dignity is amplified in a cash register honesty and philanthropic profitability is calculated and implemented to utilize the deepest human greed to produce life-saving yet highly profitable solutions.

By reading this book and practicing what is formulated here you will be in a fantastic shape to take advantage of this by being the CEO of your career and life.

As it was said in an old TV series, we have the technology!

By fairly using the technology that we do have, and by adding human intellectual capital to materials capital in each and every step that we take, we will be in a great shape to not only not do harm, but also do great good to the entire globe and its humanity.

APPENDIX Y
There is Only One of You and You Have Only One Life to Live!

Unfortunately, as an outcome of Global Financial Crisis, it seems that we are programmed. We are told you are fired, or you are laid off and we immediately do the following:

- We internalize this as if it was our fault,
- We take our heads done as if we had committed some kind of crime,
- We blame ourselves for not having something to prevent this,
- We go get those empty carton boxes and take our personal properties, our career and our lives to some extend,
- We say a half-hearted good bye to our colleagues,
- And then we leave the company premises as if we were trespassing in unfairly and undeserved self imposed shame and guilt!

In the thirty or so years as an executive coach and also a volunteer who has helped many chronic unemployed, I have learned that as bad as it might feel to lose a job, there are many good sides to it as well. Consider the following:

- As I mentioned in this book, eventually I got a job as a senior consultant reporting directly to the CEO of a major corporation with annual sales of more than $500 million dollars following the same ideas that are presented in this book.
- Since my office is directly across the hallway from the founder, I often remember one of his principles that says one needs to have fun at the job as well.
- From early on, I had learned that I do not want to do a job that I do not like or a job that I did not like.
- It is well known concept that when people do what they like money usually follows.

- You might in fact use this "down time" as being the time that you are "in between jobs". Regroup to reinvent yourself and your career.
- Rejuvenate your ties with your friends, family, and loved ones!
- Do all things that you always wanted to do that you could not when you had that miserable paycheck that took your freedom away.

- Look at it this way: you are not getting paycheck. OK the entire world will not fall apart tomorrow. You have time to re-educate yourself for a better job.
- Get active in your community. This will put you back in circulation and also will make you feel much better.
- Keep being active being active! The best antidote I know that shakes most of the being between jobs and hopeless is to keep so busy that you will forget the stupidity and pain of it all.
- Hire some tutors to teach you new things or to become better at what is your primary career.

- Give yourself a break here and there. Take daytrips; get a massage; go to all those local museums, parks, cinemas, and theaters.
- I know that you are so afraid that you counting pennies since your must be fearful about where the next dollar will come from. Nevertheless, take a vacation by going somewhere else to rewind your mind.
- Help someone else find a job.
- Help a single mom or dad to teach their kids for free.

- Look at want ads in Craig's List.
- Put ads in Craig's for potential jobs for you. I believe that this is still free.
- Offer to train others in the same field that you are. You might want to offer a few free ones until the word gets around and you get few new ones that you can charge.
- Call two or three people each day to network.
- Get a set of business cards made so people can contact you if and when they have something for you. FedEx does a good job in printing cards. There are also a lot of free software and even companies that would do this for you for free.
- Maybe start working in a desperation job situation.
- Offer to work for free for one week.
- Offer to "job share" with someone in the same primary job area that you have experience in. Many people are working so hard that would welcome this so they get a break.
- Maybe work someplace as a volunteer.

- Music and art are known to help. Listening to your favorite radio station or music will be extremely helpful and uplifting.
- Maybe you learn to play some instrument or pick up painting, or whatever turns you on.

- Get a notebook or create a file in computer to keep track of accomplishments and action items.
- You might also write your feelings in this book so the book becomes a good companion in your job search effort.

- One of the most common and regretful things is that those who are in between jobs think that they had wasted part of their lives just because they were not employed. I went through this self-damnation as well. However, if you honestly think about it, nothing is ever wasted in this huge galaxy. Not even a drop of water is wasted as it might disappear from our site and then come back in the form of rain.
- I have seen single moms or dads take the severance pay and then quickly find even a better job.
- I have seen an impressive innovation of "Momtrepreneurs or Dadtreperneurships" which is mom or dad who decides to liberate himself or herself by declaring Incorporation, and start a business using nothing more than a laptop and using the kitchen table.
- I have seen people look ten years younger and a lot of healthier by using this down time after a layoff to reinvent themselves and reinforce their careers.

- I have also seen people who insist on getting the same job as they had before where there no such a thing anymore.
- I know people who think that working means a big company hiring them and having the delusion of job security since they have a regular paycheck.
- I have also seen people who decide instead of one old-fashioned job, they might be much better off with three 1/3 jobs. Or, have a part time job in their primary career as well as a part time

222

standby while to make ends meet, have a desperation job as well.

- However, you might be asking, "How about government creating jobs for us?" Great. If the government gets you a job, even if it is not the ideal job, take it. What I am saying here is that while we are waiting for the government and politicians to help us by improving the unemployment, we need to take matters in our hands and personally create the best job we humanly can create for ourselves.

**"When your life seems dark and cold,
And, you have a dream to hold"**

These were lyrics that Petula Clark sang in her fantastic concert live in Olympia Concert Hall in Paris in 2003!
For over thirty years I have seen how layoffs can have a devastating impact on incomes, jobs, careers, families, dreams, lives, economy, and business.

A dear friend and colleague of many years told me, "Bruce, get off your soap opera! This is business. I was fired or got a layoff notice just like many kids who delivered the afternoon paper at the end of summer. I did not think of it much. Business is business; there are times managers hire and there are times they fire. What is the big deal? When there are buyers and customers and money, managers hire; when there is no money, then managers have to lay off! I have learned the game; if the company does not care for me, I do not care for the company or its customers either. I go to work; work place is toxic so I turn off my brain; as for job security, each day that I am not fired or laid off, then that day was the secure as in job security. Who cares Bruce?"

This is what, in my opinion, makes life dark and cold. We are working yet life and work is not exciting, interesting or productive. This toxicity of the work place spills over to life in general and tries to force us to let go of our dreams. This devastating and shocking force happens exactly when we need to hold to our dream even more than ever before.

"When the pain is all you see"

Studies have compared sudden job loss, layoffs, and death and found that the impact of a layoff can be somewhat comparable to a serious loss as a death in the family.

An old and wise friend was fond of saying that pain may not be optional as life is sometimes very difficult. However, he would quickly add that suffering is mostly optional!

**"And, remember, when you are gone,
Special things live on and on!"**

One of the real time heroes and role models in my life is a best friend of more than twenty years. Without any reservation I can tell that he was and is one of the best managers and professionals I had seen anywhere and anytime.

After an unhappy career with a major company he decided that family was his number one priority in life. The first chance he got, he used his Social Security benefits to provide some income so he can focus his entire life on his daughter!

When you see both of them together, you can sure see that his efforts and seemingly sacrifices have paid off and have paid off handsomely.

His daughter is a gymnast; she has great grades; and more importantly she is a happy and active eight grader. Now contrast this with my conversation with a senior executive. "Bruce, I gave the best I could to my kids; I sent them to the best European boarding schools; I worked so hard that I almost killed myself; yet, I was not there for them. They did not bond with their dad since dad was business trips half way across the world and when I was here at home, I was working day and night! They grew up in a blink of an eye. Now they have their lives and their own friends. Dad is loved, but dad is not one of their buddies or best friends!"

In late sixties, Petula Clark's "My Love" song became an international best seller. A job is a job and it will always be a job. But love for ourselves, people around us, and life can be deeper than the ocean and wider than the sky!

Hopefully, you too will have the equivalent of Petula Clark concert in making sure there is harmony in life and work; we must have a balanced life otherwise, nothing is worth it.

References:

1. Future Shock by Alvin Toffler: Summary & Study Guide
2. Too Big to Fail: The Inside Story of How Wall Street and Washington Fought to Save the Financial System--and Themselves [Paperback] Andrew Ross Sorkin
3. What Color Is Your Parachute? 2012: A Practical Manual for Job-Hunters and Career-Changers by Richard N. Bolles (Aug 16, 2011)
4. Do What You Love, The Money Will Follow: Discovering Your Right Livelihood by Marsha Sinetar (Mar 4, 1989)
5. Aftershock: Protect Yourself and Profit in the Next Global Meltdown, Second Edition, David Wiedemer, Ph D, Robert A. Wiedemer, Cindy Spitzer, John Wiley, 2011
6. Aftershocks' High Income Guide, David Wiedemer, Ph. D., Robert A. Wiedemer, Cindy Spitzer, John Wiley, 2011
7. How Starbucks Saved My Life: A Son of Privilege Learns to Live Like Everyone Else by Michael Gill (Sep 20, 2007)
8. Organizational Behavior (14th Edition) by Stephen P. Robbins and Timothy A. Judge (Jan 16, 2010)
9. Leadership: Theory and Practice by Peter Guy Northouse (Oct 26, 2006)
10. http://www.youtube.com/results?search_query=razban01&oq=razban01&aq=f&aqi=&aql=&gs_sm=s&gs_upl=10957l15377l0l207l8l8l7l0l1l0l0l242l1114l0.3.3l6l0
11. Too Big to Fail: The Inside Story of How Wall Street and Washington Fought to Save the Financial System--and Themselves by Andrew Ross Sorkin (May 11, 2011)
12. Back to Work: Why We Need Smart Government for a Strong Economy by Bill Clinton (Nov 8, 2011)
13. Capitalism 4.0: The Birth of a New Economy in the Aftermath of Crisis by Anatole Kaletsky (Jun 28, 2011)
14. The Lights in the Tunnel: Automation, Accelerating Technology and the Economy of the Future by Martin Ford (Sep 22, 2009)
15. The HP Phenomenon: Innovation and Business Transformation (Stanford Business Books) by Charles H. House
16. So Rich, So Poor: Why It's So Hard to End Poverty in America by Peter B. Edelman (May 29, 2012)
17. See You at the Top: 25th Anniversary Edition by Zig Ziglar (Jun 30, 2000)
18. Norman Vincent Peale: Three Complete Books: The Power of Positive Thinking; The Positive Principle Today; Enthusiasm Makes the Difference by Norman Vincent Peale (Sep 21, 1992)
19. I AM Wishes Fulfilled Meditation by Dr. Wayne W. Dyer and James

F. Twyman (Mar 1, 2012)

Le travail, travail, travail, travail:
Le travail en période de turbulence

Votre propre plan d'action de travail!

Bruce B. Razban, CEO, RI International, Inc.

הדובע הדובע הדובע הדובע:
הדובע בזמניס סוערים

שלך בעובדת ותכנית הפעולה!

Bruce B. Razban, CEO, RI International, Inc.

ジョブズ、ジョブズ、ジョブズ、ジョブズ：
激動の時代に働く

独自の作業行動計画！

Bruce B. Razban, CEO, RI International, Inc.

乔布斯，乔布斯，乔布斯，乔布斯：
在动荡时期

你自己的工作行动计划"！

Bruce B. Razban, CEO, RI International, Inc.